drink the harvest

MAKING AND PRESERVING
Juices, Wines, Meads, Teas, and Ciders

NAN K. CHASE
DeNEICE C. GUEST

Photographs by Johnny Autry

The mission of Storey Publishing is to serve our customers by
publishing practical information that encourages
personal independence in harmony with the environment.

EDITED BY Lisa H. Hiley and Carleen Madigan

ART DIRECTION AND BOOK DESIGN BY
Carolyn Eckert

TEXT PRODUCTION BY Liseann Karandisecky

COVER AND INTERIOR PHOTOGRAPHY BY
© Johnny Autry, except by Mars Vilaubi:
vi (top), 16, 18, 43, 52, 82, 94, 111, 112, 115
(left), 116 (steps 2–4), 117, 118, 121–124,
126, 127, 137, 139, 150, 158, 161, 165, 166,
191, 202, 212, 213, and 215; © Europe-France/
Alamy: 20; © ZUMA Press, Inc./Alamy: 26
(top); © Organics Image Library/Alamy: 26
(bottom); © Picture Library/Alamy: 33; ©
Denis Iachimovschi/123rf: 42; and © Humberto
Olarte Cupas/Flora/Alamy: 143

BACKGROUNDS CREATED BY Carolyn Eckert

PHOTO STYLING BY Charlotte Autry

INDEXED BY Nancy D. Wood

© 2014 by Nan K. Chase and DeNeice C. Guest

Be sure to read all instructions thoroughly
before using any of the techniques or recipes in this
book and follow all of the recommended safety
guidelines.

The information in this book is true and complete to the best of our knowledge. All
recommendations are made without guarantee
on the part of the author or Storey Publishing.
The author and publisher disclaim any liability in
connection with the use of this information.

Storey books are available for special premium and promotional uses and for customized
editions. For further information, please call
1-800-793-9396.

Storey Publishing
210 MASS MoCA Way
North Adams, MA 01247
www.storey.com

Printed in China by Toppan Leefung Printing Ltd.
10 9 8 7 6 5 4 3 2 1

Library of Congress Cataloging-in-Publication Data

Chase, Nan K., 1954-
  Drink the harvest / by Nan K. Chase and
DeNeice C. Guest.
      pages cm
  Includes index.
  ISBN 978-1-61212-159-8 (pbk. : alk. paper)
  ISBN 978-1-60342-913-9 (ebook) 1. Fruit juices.
  2. Vegetable juices. 3. Wine and wine making.
  4. Kitchen gardens. I. Guest, DeNeice C. II. Title.
TP562.C44 2014
663'.63--dc23

                                           2013045042

Storey Publishing is committed to making environmentally responsible manufacturing decisions.
This book was printed on paper made from sustainably harvested fiber.

drink the
harvest

WE DEDICATE this book to the inspired professionals at the Cooperative Extension System of the United States Department of Agriculture, who have been teaching gardeners and cooks for generations.

WE GRATEFULLY ACKNOWLEDGE all the older gardeners we have met through the years, for the wisdom they so eagerly share. We also appreciate the younger gardeners in our lives who bring freshness and energy into any garden. And we acknowledge our many good friends in the Asheville E-Z Gardeners, a club that's made it "E-Z" to try new things.

part 1
from garden to kitchen

part 2
juices & fermented beverages

part 3
syrups & teas

introduction

WELCOME TO THE WONDERFUL WORLD OF HOMEGROWN BEVERAGES. Beyond the edible landscape lies the "drinkable" landscape, where any fruit, any vine or berry, any herb or flower blossom may be the stuff of juice, wine, syrup, or tea.

That's where we live, where we garden, cook, and imbibe. We love sharing good times with our families and our friends, at get-togethers that are enlivened with delicious beverages from our gardens. We share a passion for putting up fruit and vegetable juices in all forms and using them in cocktails, for marinades and seasonings, in soups and salads, all sorts of places.

As part of the explosive national movement to plant and harvest food ever closer to home, we noticed that it was almost too successful! People everywhere were planting bigger and more diverse gardens, and pretty soon many gardeners were swamped with quickly ripening produce from vegetable gardens, berry patches, and orchards, not to mention the bounty from farmers' markets. What to do with it all? We agreed that someone should be talking about how fun and rewarding it is to maximize garden harvest by processing beverages, not to mention how economical.

This book is not just for experienced gardeners and expert cooks. It is for everyone who loves good food and drink, appreciates economy, embraces creativity, and wants new ideas for a memorable garden and an inviting table. This book is for:

Parents who want to limit their children's consumption of empty calories from high-fructose corn syrup while providing nutrition and encouraging an interest in good food.

Gourmet cooks looking for unique offerings for friends and guests. (Simply uncork a bottle of prickly pear cactus wine to create a sensation.)

Urban homesteaders motivated to wrest more of their diet, solid and liquid, from the streets around them.

Suburban gardeners trying to bring more utility to their spacious and well-tended yards.

Farm families with the know-how to process bulk foods and enough land to plant additional high-production crops.

Conscious eaters who insist on pure, safe foods that are free of pesticides and genetically modified organisms (GMOs) and who like to prepare their own meals from the ingredients up.

Our dream is that after trying some of these recipes and mastering the general principles, you will gain confidence, get creative, and start making up your own recipes based on the contents of your own plot of land. One of our best discoveries during our months of field research was that two of the most flavorful and productive of all the drinkable crops are also great in the home landscape: crab apples and prickly pear cactus.

Cheers!

[signature] and *[signature]*

1

part 1

from garden to kitchen

1

finding beverages in your garden

Are you ready to take your garden to an amazing level of productivity? Ready to use more of what you grow and fill your larder with joy? Ready to taste fruits and vegetables, herbs and flowers as you never have before? Ready for something new, something unusual in the kitchen?

Then come along and join us as we explore a world of homegrown beverages that's waiting just outside your door, a world of delicious, nutritious drinks to enjoy fresh or to put up by canning or fermenting or freezing so you can savor them all year long.

We'll show you how to capture your garden's bounty at its peak and eliminate the waste that sometimes accompanies extra-big crops. We'll give you tips on planning and planting your garden with drinkable crops, everything from wildflowers to watermelons, and carrots to crab apples. And we'll help you extend the harvest season no matter where you live.

As with any other cookbook, this volume is a starting point for your own experimentation. There's no limit to what you can do with beverages.

the joys
of juice
(and other drinks)

IMAGINE STARTING YOUR DAY with a breakfast that includes a serving of jewel-colored berry juice. For lunch or an afternoon snack, add a dose of good health with a glass of spiced apple cider. Cocktail hour might feature a Bloody Mary (or nonalcoholic Virgin Mary) made with vegetables from the backyard, or a homemade rice wine flavored with fresh organic citrus. Serve rich honey-toned mead or well-aged grape wine with dinner, then settle in for the evening with a cup of herbal tea.

You can "grow" all these drinks and many more, plus intriguing flavored syrups to add to other beverages. Most can come from a single garden, once you learn to spot the beverage potential of familiar plants and understand how even a few new plant selections will greatly expand your beverage choices.

Don't worry, though. You don't need a big yard with lots of fruit trees, row upon row of berry bushes or grape vines, dozens of tomato plants, and other summer vegetables. And we know that not everyone has access to endless herbs, rose bushes galore, and unusual specimens like prickly pear cactus and lemons.

Even *we* don't have all those goodies in our gardens, although we do grow enough of them to have tasted and experimented with them while creating the recipes in this book. Like so many others who love to cook and eat fresh food, we supplement our homegrown produce with bulk quantities from local farmers' markets. And like gardeners everywhere, we have gardening friends who like to share their best, most prolific crops while these foods are at the peak of ripeness.

Community-supported agriculture (CSA) shares and pick-your-own farms can also round out the supply side. It's perfectly all right to stock up on picked-this-morning ingredients to use in crafting your own close-to-homegrown beverages. The freshness factor is nearly the same, and so are the flavor and nutrition.

If your growing conditions are not ideal, you can make the best of what you do have. Maybe you can grow a few potted plants; fresh basil and Meyer lemons are well suited for syrups or wine. If you have a small yard with one or two old-yet-productive fruit trees and not much else, that's fine, too. It may well happen that your limited selection of plants will make terrific beverages; plum wine and pear cider are just two examples that might fit the bill. Perhaps your yard is wooded and damp; if so, it's perfect for growing wildflowers, such as nettles and bee balm, that make flavorful and beneficial teas.

where's the juice?

NO MATTER WHAT'S already growing in your garden, this book suggests ways to use as much as you can pick, pluck, snip, or dig. You'll notice that we talk a lot about actual cooking, not just about dropping ingredients in a blender and flipping the switch (although there are a few recipes like that) and not just about plopping fruits or herbs into alcohol to create instant bar drinks (although there is one recipe like that). We talk about processing fruits, vegetables, herbs, wildflowers, and even tree sap in different ways and then using these products for further processing and long-term storage. This book describes several methods in detail.

juice extraction

Extraction is a way to harvest the liquid that is bound up in fresh fruits such as peaches, pears, apples, and grapes, and in more unusual fare like prickly pear cactus fruits and service-berries. Separating the juice from fibrous solids is the necessary first step for making shelf-stable nonalcoholic beverages and syrups as well as wine, mead, and hard cider.

We recommend two main methods, according to the quantity of fruit you have and the equipment on hand: (1) heat extraction by cooking whole or chopped fruit in filtered water, then straining it, and (2) cold-processing by pressing chunks of fruit in a screw-driven press.

Some of our recipes call for two methods to eliminate waste in fruit processing. For instance, after you've finished pressing grapes, pears, or apples in a heavy-duty fruit press to make cider, you can make lighter juices by boiling the leftover pulp and straining that juice.

WHY FILTERED WATER?

Note that all our recipes involving heat extraction and fermentation call for filtered water. Why? Using filtered water minimizes any unpleasant off-tasting characteristics that could settle in the finished product: salts, metals, chlorine, minerals, bacteria, anything. What you are striving for in homegrown beverages is the flavor of the fresh ingredients and nothing else.

There are several options for filtering water: pitcher-style filter charcoal systems, filters built into kitchen faucets, or stand-alone drinking water systems with five-gallon jugs of water. We don't recommend using distilled water for two reasons: We don't like the taste and it has had important components removed in processing. Thus, distilled water can react badly with yeast and cause fermentation failures.

The variety

of recipes in this book is intended as a starting point to encourage you to think outside the juice box.

honey instead of sugar), hard ciders from various fruits, and an Italian-style lemon liqueur.

Fermentation follows a few basic principles and is just as easy as making bread; equipment needn't be complicated or expensive, and the fermentation requires almost no added energy and few extra ingredients. These methods take time more than effort, and can give a long-term focus to your future garden endeavors.

evaporation

Cooking down liquids on the stovetop is an easy way to turn homemade juices into scrumptious syrups that can be used for anything from topping pancakes to flavoring cocktails. We have created unusual but tasty combinations of fruits, herbs, and spices that will tickle your taste buds while using some of the bits and pieces from the garden that you may not have used before. Watermelon syrup, anyone?

fermentation

Winemaking and other fermentation methods can work magic with fruit, of course, but also with vegetables, herbs, and even flowers. Practically everyone has heard of dandelion wine, but you can make wine from potatoes or parsley, too. We provide easy recipes that will let you try stretching the yield of almost anything from the garden. In addition to wine, we've included recipes for mead (much like wine, but made with

canning

Canning fresh fruits and vegetables is like capturing summer in a jar. After a long growing season, it's gratifying in so many ways to stock the pantry with jars of brightly colored, delicious food and drink. This method is safe, easy, and economical, although it can be hot work.

Canning (i.e., vacuum-sealing food or beverages in tempered glass jars) lets you save lots and lots of your harvest for a year or more, and there's no chance that a power failure will ruin your hard work, as can happen with freezing. A few generations ago cooks commonly included canning in their kitchen repertoire, but the practice waned with the advent of refrigeration and the spread of grocery stores. We love how canning is making a comeback, and we'll provide lots of information about doing it yourself.

dehydration

Plant material can be dried quickly with an electric or, in arid and sunny climates, a solar, dehydrator. Herbs, flowers, and black and green teas all lend themselves to dehydrating, since the results retain their flavor and store well. By drying some of your garden harvest at the peak of freshness, often in spring, you can preserve it immediately for use a year or more later.

In this book you'll find many recipes for wines, meads, and teas that call for herbs. Dehydration can be a convenient way to stretch the seasons. Dry the herbs now and make the wine later, when some of the other ingredients are ripe.

freezing

Freezing is a quick, easy way to preserve beverages, and it works especially well for small batches. Sometimes it is the best method to use as an intermediate step: freeze some juice or even the unprocessed fruit, and then thaw it later to make further recipes. Berries, for instance, come ripe in small batches. You can freeze enough berries over a few weeks to eventually make juice, mead, or syrup.

you have the skills

IF YOU CAN DO a little bit of weeding in the garden every day that weather permits, and if you can take a pair of kitchen scissors and a harvest basket along, you already have the skills to produce homegrown beverages. It's that easy!

If you can boil water and turn on a dishwasher, and if you can set a timer and use measuring cups, you already have the skills to produce homegrown beverages. It's that easy!

Throw in the willingness to dedicate time to processing crops as they reach optimum conditions, and you're almost there. One key to making the kind of homegrown beverages that win state fair ribbons and cost just pennies per

SOLAR DEHYDRATORS

Solar-powered food dehydrators may not work in all parts of the United States, but in sunny climates they may be a great option for preserving herbs, blossoms, and fruits. It's not difficult to build a solar-powered dehydrator from plans readily found online.

Combining good

garden management and careful kitchen habits through the growing season is the only secret to the marvelous realm of grow-them, make-them drinks.

serving is follow-through: when grapes or berries are ripe, they are ripe for only a short time, so pick and process them without delay. We'll talk a little bit about garden management shortly, but first let's turn to the kitchen side of the equation.

If you have never canned anything or never made wine, you're definitely not alone. We've outlined the steps as plainly as we can and have been as accurate as possible about total processing time. A number of our recipes call for liquids to stand overnight for best results; knowing that will help your planning and reduce stress. In other words, the cooking itself may not take long, but preparation and waiting can add to the overall time considerably. It's nice to know just how many hours to block out of your busy week.

You may be wondering what kind of kitchen layout you need. We know

cooks who have designed large kitchens especially for their canning and brewing activities, with double sinks, double dishwashers, extra-big ranges, and miles of shelving. We also know accomplished cooks and winemakers with tiny kitchens, no dishwasher, a midsize stove, and only an undercounter fridge with a freezer the size of an egg carton. Some cooks in hot regions rig up seasonal open-air kitchens to help beat the heat; these often rudimentary kitchens can be highly functional. All the recipes in this book can work in any size kitchen as long as you organize countertop space efficiently and keep washing and putting away utensils as you work.

What matters most in making and preserving beverages at home is sanitation: clean surfaces and tools and vessels, plus carefully washed fruit and vegetables. Juice extraction, canning, and fermentation really are easy, but your safety and drinking pleasure depend on encouraging the good kind of chemical reactions and discouraging the bad. Be prepared to use a lot of scalding hot water as you try the recipes in this book. It's a must, so take precautions with appropriate clothing and safety equipment to avoid burns.

your garden's already perfect

YOUR GARDEN IS PERFECT because it is full of potential, the potential for growth and change. It might not seem perfect today, but tomorrow all you have to do is make one improvement, take one little step toward more beverage production. And the next day, one more step. It could be deadheading herbs so they grow thicker, or pruning suckers from around fruit trees so the yield improves, or pulling up spent vegetable plants for the compost pile. It could be mulching tomatoes or planting fennel seeds in peat pots for transplant later in the season.

The point is not to feel overwhelmed. The reality of creating and putting up beverages is that if you try to do it all at once, making every recipe you possibly can, using every bit of homegrown and other locally grown produce available, it will overwhelm you.

Your garden may even include a stretch of otherwise abandoned roadside or an untended lot that holds some culinary treasure within its gritty, weedy, trash-bedecked swale. In the search for free edible produce, we always keep an eye on that unexpected treasure of a specimen until it is ripe and ready to pick. This occasional hunter-gatherer approach has served us well with such useful crops as pear, quince, apple and crab apple, mint, prickly pear, serviceberry, and blackberry, to name just a few. These plants may grow wild in your area, or you may have neighbors with an abundance to share.

make it work for you

As you begin to nurture a homegrown beverage garden and make wonderful drinks from the harvest, you may find, as we have, that it's so much fun, so interesting and rewarding, that you want to expand your efforts. Start by evaluating your available space in terms of production value, that is, how many quarts of fruit juice or vegetable juice, how many bottles of wine or mead, how many gallons of cider or pints of syrup each square foot might yield at maturity and in the best growing conditions.

Two ways to help make choices in plant selection and placement are to consider the scale of the operations you envision and to estimate the time required to maintain a garden of that size, harvest the crops, and process everything. For planning the scale, chapter 2 gives more detail about the plants that go into making beverages and their most favorable growing conditions, but the following are the general categories:

Herbs. Snip and use within just a few minutes of planting (if you buy them already grown in pots) or a few weeks (if you buy seeds or seedlings). Depending on the herb, you can count on months or years of steady production.

11

1. potato; 2. red cabbage; 3. chamomile; 4. sunflower (ornamental);
5. cherry tomatoes; 6. chard; 7. persimmon; 8. coral bells (ornamental)

Vegetables. Yields can begin in just a few months and, depending on the plant, continue for weeks on end through the growing cycle, whether spring, summer, or fall. Some exceptional specimens, including many greens, can grow and produce much of the year.

Fruiting vines and berry bushes. Depending on the size, number of plants, and age, berries can provide a great yield, with lots of flavor. Yield increases as the plants age; it may be three years or so before full production is available.

Orchard fruits. Here's the potential for big yields and volume production, but with the possibility, too, of waiting five years or more before that happens.

Trees and shrubs. Investments in the future, trees and shrubs can help anchor a productive garden. Handsome trees like maple and birch yield sap that can be processed into delicious beverages, and indeed we include a recipe for birch sap wine (using, it's true, a jar of store-bought "birch water"). Currant, gooseberry, serviceberry, blackberry, huckleberry, even blueberry bushes have landscape value, as do some dwarf citrus.

Be realistic:

If space is tight inside and out, your entire scale of operations may need to be small. If you have the luxury of a large yard and spacious cupboards, then by all means, think big.

1. paw paw tree; 2. lavender; 3. chard

If you are just starting out with gardening and food production, you will have to gain experience in growing plants of all kinds. If you have been gardening for years, you may be eager to grow new varieties of old favorites or add a new category. Whatever your choices, remember that nurturing, harvesting, and processing fresh garden ingredients can go on practically throughout the year, no matter where you live. Different fruits, vegetables, berries, and herbs start producing at different rates, so it may take several years to fully develop a beverage garden and reap a satisfactory harvest of mature ingredients.

Finally, scale refers not just to the size of your garden but also to your work space and, at least as important, your storage space. You'll need room for all those big bowls, for various tools, for canning jars and wine bottles, for a fruit press or an immersion blender, for dehydrating equipment, and for frozen beverages.

JOIN A GARDEN CLUB!

Garden clubs are found in every part of the country and welcome everyone, young or old, experienced or newbie. This is gardening at its most educational and informal, with plenty of community gardening activities and lots of new people to meet. See www.gardenclub.org for the location of a club near you.

2

growing a beverage garden

We'd like to introduce you to the plants we used to create the recipes in this book, and to list some of the strengths and drawbacks of each. You may already grow some of them or wish to add others that produce exceptionally well in your locale. Read through the recipes and imagine how the crops we mention might fit into your own beverage garden to make it both more productive and more beautiful.

Here's something important we have learned: The official hardiness zone of any plant matters far less than the microclimate where you plant it, and the zones can be stretched quite a bit. We believe that most of the plants we mention here can grow successfully in most of the United States and in some parts of Canada.

Your selection of homegrown beverages will certainly change over the course of several years, expanding ever outward as more and more plants come on line. You may be surprised to find you have to thin out the garden earlier than you thought possible, in order to free up space for the strongest performers and consign lesser specimens to the giveaway list, the plant exchange, or even the compost pile.

meet our favorite plants

apple

ALTHOUGH WE LIST our favorite plants here alphabetically within categories, read carefully: some of our strongest recommendations may surprise you.

orchard fruits

Apples. Apples are great in many ways, and especially important in beverage production, but we recommend leaving them primarily to commercial growers, not because apples are difficult to grow but because it takes so much fruit and some years of care to produce any appreciative amount of beverages (though once you have enough apples on hand, the cider and juice will flow). Unless you have a lot of room for planting or already possess a mature bearing tree, grow apples for eating or baking; for beverages use ones from pick-your-own orchards, abandoned properties, or farmers' markets. Apples make wonderful juice, cider, wine, and mead.

crab apple

peach

Crab apples. A must-have in any size beverage garden, crab apples are our number one favorite! In particular, the Callaway variety and to some extent the Kerr are perfect for beginning fruit aficionados. The trees, which are in fact members of the rose family, are pest- and disease-resistant, early to bear fruit, copious producers, and easy to maintain, since they require little pruning and virtually no spraying. The sweet-tart little apples yield amazing quantities of juice per gallon of fruit, and the gorgeous blossoms, ranging from white to deep pink, attract lots of pollinating insects. In addition to the traditional jelly, crab apples make lovely juice, mead, and wine.

Lemons, oranges, grapefruits. In America's semitropical zones, citrus trees are a no-brainer. But in cooler regions, do consider taking them on as conservatory plants or at the very least fair-weather outdoor plants that overwinter indoors. Hand-pollinated and adequately fertilized, dwarf citrus trees in pots can produce plenty of succulent fruits for beverages and can do so without sprays, waxes, or other chemicals on the skins. The life cycle of a lemon, from bloom to table, may be as long as a year. The fruits can become almost like a group of friends as you watch them develop. Citrus fruits can be turned into wine, mead, and liqueur, plus syrup, and tea.

Peaches. Finicky about growing conditions, peach trees require confident major pruning every year and don't live long, commonly just 15 or 20 years. They often need lots of spraying to contain diseases, which can run rampant over tree and fruit. But go ahead and try them if you have a long growing season, plus good air circulation and plenty of water available. Or buy high-quality peaches in bulk whenever they're available from nearby farms, usually in late spring and early summer. The versatile juice is useful for fruit juice combinations, wine, and syrups.

Pears. Considering how unjuicy pears can be when you bite into them, this favorite Old World fruit yields large quantities of juice. The most prolific pear trees defy logic. On the one hand, they may thrive without pruning or without an apparent mate for pollination, but when pampered they sometimes fail to grow. On the other hand, their supple young branches make them

BUY LOCAL

Although large discount garden centers may have a lot of selection, the plants may not be grown anywhere near your own soil and weather conditions. If you buy locally grown plant starts, you are more likely to have success in severe conditions in your area. The locally grown plants will already be acclimated and can put on more robust growth in a hurry.

A GALLON OF FRUIT?

It may sound odd to measure whole fruit and berries by the gallon, but we find it simplest to measure a dry gallon of fruit by eyeballing it, comparing a volume of fruit to the volume of a gallon milk jug, or we use bowls that hold two gallons and take it from there.

raspberry

blueberry

excellent candidates for training onto an espalier. Espaliered pears don't take up much room, and growing them against a warm, dry wall can help prevent some disease problems. Always worth a try, pears make a good basic beverage crop for juice, cider, and syrups.

berries and vines

Blackberries, raspberries, and other bramble fruits. Known loosely as bramble fruits, a lot of the plants with the name "berry" share common characteristics. They produce succulent, deliciously tart, and tasty fruit that makes memorable beverages: juice mixes, wine, mead, syrups, and leaf teas. They can start bearing in just a few years but will always require pruning and thinning, and sometimes need support structures to help maximize yield. Berries can thrive on thin rocky soil that's generally dry, but they need extra water to help set fruit; in cold climates they should be mulched with straw in winter.

Blueberries. If you can grow blueberries, plant as many bushes as possible. Their nutritional value tops the

charts, and their flavor is a thing of wonder. In big enough quantities, blueberries can be turned into pure juice for canning, as well as into mead, tea, and syrups. The bushes favor acid soil, loose and sloping, and can take cold weather. They need at least three or four years to get established and must be sited with care; netting helps offset losses from birds. These splendid landscape bushes blush crimson in the fall. At top production, a mature blueberry bush might yield a gallon of berries per season.

Currants. We recommend currants for carefree, high-yield fruit with lots of vitamin C and terrific flavor. The shrubs tend to spread quickly if left untended. Note that currants are not legal to grow in all states, as they can serve as a host to pests that damage commercial white pine operations.

Grapes. Here's a fine garden companion, a vine that with minimal care and little special treatment may yield many pounds of fruit annually after just a few years. Once established, grapes do need a firm, consistent hand with pruning, but they are so tough and forgiving in

serviceberry

nearly any climate that they can bounce back from beginners' mistakes. We like grapes for juice, of course, but some of the skins, preserved by refrigeration or dehydration, are useful in winemaking and other fermenting projects. Different regions have their own specialty grapes which perform best in local conditions, so take the time to source vines carefully.

Serviceberries. Also known as Juneberry, shadbush, and half a dozen other names, this small tree is native to much of North America and bears loads of reddish-purple berries with a flavor and texture much like blueberries, though a bit more grainy and with less juice. The spectacular white flowers in spring and the brilliant fall color make serviceberry valuable in the landscape. With the dark red berries you can make anything liquid; the juice is dark blue, nearly purple.

Strawberries. Well-tended strawberries can boost beverage production significantly, which is helpful if you have a bumper crop. Strawberries go from ripe to overripe very quickly,

and processing them as juice is a good way to prevent a large quantity from going to waste. The berries, when cooked and strained, yield a great deal of juice that's useful in making fruit juice combinations, frozen treats, wine, syrup, and party punch. For best results, remove all flower buds in the first year to force bigger berries the second year; after that, renew plants regularly. If you don't have space for rows, low-growing strawberries can be an effective edging in urban or suburban yards. They need a lot of water but must have good drainage to prevent disease.

SOME OF OUR NOT-SO-FAVORITES

CHERRY TREES are challenging because (unless on dwarf root stock) they quickly grow tall, putting the fruit out of reach. And birds can strip a tree of tasty ripe cherries in no time.

KIWI VINES can be difficult to grow to fruiting size because they require a male and female and *lots* of start-up time, plus room to roam.

PLUMS can easily overproduce, which is a headache if you aren't poised to process all that ripe fruit immediately; rotting fruit on the ground can not only attract ankle-level bees and wasps and nocturnal critters but also leave a mess of squashy remnants to throw away.

quince

other possibilities

Quince. Quince bushes are unobtrusive and sometimes appear, loaded with autumn fruit, along fences. Related to apples and pears, quinces boil down to fine juice and combine with other fruit juices, giving them a rich, cinnamon-tinged tone.

Rhubarb. The edible stalks of this perennial plant constitute the "fruit" of rhubarb, while the leaves are discarded (and in fact are toxic). Tart but saturated with other flavors, processed rhubarb can add its juice to spring beverage combos, as well as flavoring wine and syrup. Heavy feeders, rhubarb roots should be sited with care so that they don't need to be moved during their usual 10- to 15-year life span.

Watermelon. If you have plenty of room for these sprawling vines among all your other garden goodies, by all means grow watermelons. If you can't keep up with eating them fresh, create watermelon juices and syrups to keep the summertime experience alive, or experiment with watermelon wine!

BARTER FOR BARGAINS

See if a local farmer might let you have produce at extra-low prices if you agree to deliver a few jars of juice or bottles of wine or syrup from that produce at the end of the season. Or arrange to swap excess from your garden for something a friend or neighbor has too much of. A barter arrangement can be good for everyone.

vegetables

Beets. A useful and easy-to-grow root crop with handsome leaves on dark red stems, beets can be included in vegetable drinks.

Carrots. Harvest young carrots to add lots of vitamins to vegetable beverages.

Celeriac. A big-root form of celery, celeriac imparts a deep, aromatic tone to some herb wines and other beverages.

Potatoes. Grow your own potatoes for the most flavorful version of an unusual potato wine. With white potatoes' high potassium level, the wine has a big kick.

Tomatoes. When you and everyone you know are overrun with tomatoes, you can combine different varieties for super-duper vegetable drinks to can or freeze. Mix cherry tomatoes, heirlooms, and hybrids to obtain complex flavor highlights in juice, wine, and mead.

herbs

Basil. The midsummer magic of this aromatic garden favorite contributes to some rich mead recipes. Its flavor also enhances wines, juices, and syrups.

Bay leaf. The bay tree is flexible in the garden as a hedge, topiary, potted indoor-outdoor plant, or full-size tree, depending on climate. The leaf can be a component in syrups and vegetable juices as well as in wines and mead.

Bee balm. Magnificent with its deep red crown-shaped blooms, bee balm makes tangy, minty tea and can be used to flavor wine, mead, and syrups. It does well in wet, shady ground.

There's no need to grow all your fruits and vegetables in straight lines; they grow just as well placed throughout more natural planting arrangements.

garlic

Cardamom. An important flavoring in some syrups and other recipes, cardamom can be raised indoors if you don't live in a tropical zone. Harvest the seeds for their delicately spicy-sweet flavor.

Cayenne pepper. Just a few cayenne pepper plants can supply all the heat you need in beverages. They are easy to grow in full sun and you can use both the flesh and the seeds.

Celery. A good advanced plant for cooks, homegrown celery requires lots of fertilizer and plenty of mulch and moisture. Note, too, that it takes quite a while for celery seed to germinate.

Chamomile. This happy mass of flowers may be an annual or perennial. It makes fragrant tea and adds a lovely billowing effect in the garden.

Fennel. Handsome in the garden and quite hardy, bronze fennel has flavorful seeds following bold yellow blooms, while the tasty bulbous stalks of green or Florence fennel are useful in vegetable beverages.

Garlic. Sow garlic cloves in midautumn for harvest the following year; use the cloves in some vegetable beverages.

Ginger. A kitchen workhorse, especially in mead and wine recipes, ginger grows in tropical climates or potted, indoors, at 75°F temperatures. Fresh ginger can be made into tea, syrup, or mead.

parsley

Horseradish. This homely perennial root crop, used in vegetable drinks, deserves its own place in the garden, preferably in a moist corner where it can stay mostly undisturbed.

Lemon balm. An ingredient in relaxing teas, this mint-family member looks bright and fresh in the garden; keep it cut back to encourage thick, compact growth, and harvest it frequently. It makes a delicious, delicately flavored tea and can be used in wine, mead, and syrups.

Mint. Useful in teas, wines, and many other beverages, mint can cover a lot of ground with roots that run and spread, and it does well in moist conditions. Keep it carefully contained and harvest it freely.

Mustard seed. Fast and easy to grow, mustard supplies tangy edible leaves and lots of seed for culinary uses, including in juice, wine, and mead.

Parsley. Patience pays off with this fine crop, as seed germination is protracted and parsley grows slowly but steadily. The herb makes good wine.

Passionflower. This vine produces absolutely beautiful flowers, which, fresh or dried, go into teas and wine as well as into syrups. The flavor is sweet and light. Do not confuse passionflower with the passion fruit.

other crops

Birch trees. In far northern climates, where birch trees grow in sufficient numbers, it is possible to harvest the thin sap (also called birch water) by tapping mature trees in late winter and early spring, much like maples. Birch syrup requires large quantities of the dilute sap, a ratio of about 100:1, but an unusual and delicious birch wine needs only a gallon of birch water. Or process the sap in jars and use as a tasty tonic.

Honey. If you have been successful with bees, count on using your own honey to sweeten some juices and make the alcoholic beverage called mead. Otherwise, find a local beekeeper who sells honey in volume.

Prickly pear cactus. The fruits of this tough wildflower, called apples or tunas, look like nothing else on the planet. Glowing dark fuchsia or magenta, almost iridescent, they sit atop the plant's paddle-shaped leaves like space creatures. Prickly on the outside, the egg-sized fruits are filled with sweet, juicy pulp that is rich in vitamin C, dietary fiber, and magnesium, and has appreciable levels of calcium, potassium, and even iron.

It may take some years for clumps of the cactus to get large enough to produce usable quantities of juice and the spiny tunas need special handling, but we rate prickly pear our number two favorite (after crab apples) because it's so versatile and because you need only a few tunas to make a nice health drink.

Rose. Not so very hard to grow, especially rugosa varieties, roses produce fruits called hips that have high vitamin C content. Using the hips to make tea is a well-known practice, and the petals can be used to make wine. Roses need, above all, to have free circulation of air around the canes, balanced nutrition, and deep watering on a regular basis. In the fall, as the leaves turn, rugosa roses insert gold highlights into the garden.

Tea (*Camellia sinensis*). Though primarily familiar as an ornamental in North America, the camellia genus also includes this species, which allows you to grow your own cuppa. Tea bushes require a few years to produce enough young leaves and shoots to harvest. They can take light frost, with some varieties surviving quite low temperatures. Plant en mass as a hedge if you really want to enjoy homegrown black or green tea. (See also page 204.)

IF YOU CAN'T PICK your own prickly pears but are intrigued by this super fruit, you can order them online, in which case they will arrive with the spines removed, as shown here.

LOOKING AT THE SEASONS

Let's look at a year of seasons, to get a feel for the timeline of making homegrown beverages.

LATE WINTER, EARLY SPRING. Now is the time to start cool-weather seeds such as beets, mustard, parsley, carrots, leeks, and onions directly in the soil. The plants will mature slowly through the spring and summer. Start warmer-weather seeds such as fennel, basil, cayenne pepper, and chamomile indoors or on a warm porch, in individual peat pots for later transplant in the garden. Plant rhubarb roots.

SPRING AND EARLY SUMMER. Put seeds for celeriac and other midsummer ripening vegetables in the ground. While the soil is still cool and moist, it's not too late to transplant some roots, such as horseradish and various mints. Plant watermelon seeds, and thin fruit from orchard trees to foster healthy fruit set. Plant potatoes, and transplant any early vegetable seedlings. Harvest and process peaches and berries. Tend to herbs and harvest them as needed. Pick and process serviceberries. Start some herb wines.

MIDSUMMER. Make sure roses have enough food and water, and keep the canes cleared of weeds so that they get lots of air circulation; the hips will ripen in late fall. Keep herbs weeded, and put cayenne peppers in the ground. Keep parsley cool. This is the season for processing berry crops and peaches. Keep all your plants weeded, and water them regularly. Continue to harvest and process herbs. Start herb wines, flower wines, and meads.

LATE SUMMER, EARLY FALL. Grapes ripen and need to be pressed or boiled for juice and wine. Process herbs and flowers, drying them to use as tea or in wines and syrups. Clear out the vegetable garden, and replant it with seeds for cooler weather. Can all tomato and vegetable juices, and start picking and processing apples, crab apples, pears, and plums. Use surplus juices to make syrups with fresh or dried herbs. Begin light pruning to lighten branches after fruit bearing. Plant garlic and leeks.

LATE FALL, EARLY WINTER. Harvest and process late crops, such as prickly pear and quince, and begin harvesting citrus for limoncello. Plant all new fruit trees, vines, and berries in the late fall so that they have extra time to establish root systems before winter. Prune grapes once leaves have fallen and hard frost sets in. Harvest and process rose hips.

DEEP WINTER. Turn attention to citrus, hand-pollinating with a brush if trees stay indoors for the winter. Water and fertilize citrus trees, and repot so they have lots of room to expand. Read seed and plant catalogs and order for timely delivery in early spring.

From there it's just a matter of what grows well and with most promise the first year, and then continuing to plant more and more of the same, while also learning the techniques that favor your highest-yielding crops.

pruning for production

THE LORE OF PRUNING fruiting trees and shrubs can and does fill many books, and it's easy to get intimidated by this rather complicated subject. In this book we merely demystify pruning for beverage gardening and give you the basics. Pruning is necessary to improve the quality and quantity of fruit production: it encourages vigorous root growth, removes excess growth that saps energy from fruit development, keeps the branch structure strong and open to air and sunlight, and keeps ripe fruit within easy reach. Patient and skillful pruning can bring even old, overgrown fruit trees back into production.

Pruning needn't be difficult, but it should be methodical. Most important, take care not to overdo it: Heavy pruning too early will simply delay the onset of regular fruiting. With berries the principle is generally to encourage fresh canes or branches every year by removing aging, nonproducing ones, while with grapes the idea is to remove the vines completely except for a few buds every year to force lots of new fruiting growth.

However, even experts disagree about pruning young fruit trees and fruiting shrubs and vines when you plant them; some say to trim them substantially,

WHEN PRUNING, always use bypass pruners rather than anvil pruners, which crush live branches. Cut at a downward angle to shed water and avoid rotting.

while others recommend not pruning at all (or making just little cosmetic nips) until the plants start bearing fruit. We subscribe to the latter practice. Once the plants are established, though, we like to think of pruning as *carefully* giving fruit trees and berry bushes and grape vines a haircut every year during the dormant season.

Apples and crab apples, peaches, plums, and pears all have slightly different shaping requirements. Apples, for example, need a stable, long-term approach to pruning that encourages well-defined upright and horizontal components. Peach trees, in particular, require almost a third of the limbs to be pruned away from the center and tops every year. Start your research with the planting instructions that come with any new specimens, and follow the recommended steps.

No matter what, select pruning tools that match the job, from pruning shears that fit comfortably in your hand, to limb loppers and pruning saws, to pole pruners that use springs and ropes. Keep all tools sharp and clean, to spare insult to the plants and promote fast healing. And clean your tools often, using rubbing alcohol in cases of disease outbreaks.

a word about thinning fruit

It sounds counterintuitive to try to produce better fruit by taking away some buds, but that's the size of it. Unpruned fruit trees may produce many times more fertilized flowers, and subsequently young fruits, than the root and branch structures can possibly support year after year, and as a result the fruit does not develop to full size or the branches may actually split.

Nature often produces a fruit drop early in the season, around June, when a lot of the tiny new fruits fall off overnight; commercial apple growers may imitate this phenomenon with applications of hormones. So don't worry if a lot of fruit suddenly disappears. If your fruit trees are setting fruit too densely, you may manually pinch off enough fruiting buds to leave six inches or so in between remaining fruit.

harvesting and preparation

It's almost time to start cooking, juicing, pressing, fermenting, dehydrating, freezing, and otherwise creating some wonderful garden-to-bottle beverages. You've planted herbs, started vegetable seeds, put grape vines and berry bushes in the ground, and invested some time and love on young (or old) fruit trees. Maybe you've even put a few dwarf citrus trees into pots. If you aren't currently growing anything at all but are instead buying all your produce, that's fine, too. Our recipes will work no matter what sources you use.

Whatever your passion, whatever the size of your garden (or your local farmers' market), using the right equipment and the right approach to picking and handling fresh ingredients will help you achieve great results. When you use cleaned and sorted top-quality fruit and vegetables, herbs and flowers (all harvested at peak flavor) you can serve your beverages with pride and confidence.

reaping what you've sown

THERE'S SOMETHING SPECIAL about seeing a completed batch of berry juice or flower wine, even a small batch, lined up on the kitchen counter. All the hot afternoons of weeding the vegetables, all the anguish of a late spring frost, all the happiness of picking an armload of fragrant herbs . . . why, you're bottling memories!

And when you share your homegrown beverages with your family and your closest friends, those occasions become memorable, too. Breakfast, lunch, dinner, and all the drinkable moments in between can showcase your new-found talents. And when it comes to the fermented beverages wine and mead, your expertise develops steadily over the years while your first efforts mellow in the bottle.

Then there's the sheer beauty of the finished products, especially when they are processed and preserved in glass jars. You'll notice that almost all our recipes suggest canning rather than freezing if there's more than you have room for in the fridge. Although freezing works perfectly well as a pre-servative, too often, alas, items that go into the freezer never emerge. Out of sight, out of mind. Canning is safe and simple, and since canned goods don't need to be thawed they are always ready to use.

The beverages made from the recipes in this book are very lovely, and, as you will find out, more saturated with natural flavor than almost anything you can buy at a grocery store. There's almost no sugar added in many of our recipes, which means that you taste fruit juice and blended vegetables and herbs as they were picked, *not* high-fructose corn syrup or other flavor sub-stitutes that are devoid of nutritional content. The same goes for salt; in some cases we recommend just a bit to help canned beverages retain their color and freshness, but otherwise we generally ignore it.

IT'S FUN to package your wine, mead, and syrups in decorative bottles if you can afford it, but recycled bottles are perfectly appropriate, as long as they are properly sealed. It's a joy to open a cupboard full of color, but once you open a bottle, refrigerate any remaining beverage.

is it ripe yet?

THE FRESHNESS FACTOR is hard to describe but you know it when you see it, smell it, and taste it. That apple is *just* right. Yet there's more to harvesting crops for beverage production than merely choosing a pretty piece of fruit. An apple that's ripe enough to pluck from the tree and eat out of hand — crunchy, juicy, and sweet — may not be the best apple for cider.

In fact, apple experts recommend letting a big pile of apples age outdoors for several weeks before pressing them into cider. The resting period allows moisture to escape from the fruit, which concentrates the flavor. Furthermore, cider makers say that mixing several different apple types in one batch, including tart ones, is essential for a well-balanced drink.

Pears, though closely related to apples, behave quite differently. They can be harvested while still green and hard, then chopped and pressed for shockingly large quantities of delicate juice. If pears are left too long, until they are completely soft on the tree, the sugars may have morphed into something less desirable and microorganisms on the skin could compromise fermentation. And so it goes among all the beverage-friendly plants, each displaying its own version of ripeness. We try in the chapters that follow to point out cases that need particular attention to special timing or handling.

A complex interplay of natural sugars, in the case of fruits and berries, and the development of flavor-bearing oils, in the case of herbs, means that harvesting a single crop may not occur all at once. There's so much variety in the plant world that your entire harvest period may last for much of the year, while the harvest period of any one plant may run from just a few days to several weeks.

With berries, for example, the ripening comes a little bit every day for a few weeks, so it's difficult to collect enough at once if you don't have a lot of plants. In that case freeze the small daily batches and accumulate enough for a standard recipe, or at the very least refrigerate them dry, without washing, to hold them. In fact, most fruit should only be washed just before being processed, to prevent bruising and rot.

GARDEN CALENDAR

Why not dedicate an extra wall calendar to your garden operations? Even if you only have a postage-stamp yard, marking to-do dates on a calendar helps regulate the work flow of planting, harvesting, and processing. For planting dates in your area, consult gardening books, magazines, or websites such as *Mother Earth News*, or find a "When to Plant" app.

The way you cut

and handle your crops determines your efficiency. The more carefully you treat plants from harvest through washing, the less you waste.

Two quarts of fruit is about the minimum quantity for any recipe, and most of ours start with approximately a gallon of fruit or berries (see A Gallon of Fruit?, page 17). In our experience, a flat (12 pints) of berries is the minimum practical quantity. For bulky crops, including peaches, tomatoes, and apples, we often suggest a minimum of 15 pounds; there's virtually no upper limit, except for the size of your cookware and bowls.

picking and washing

Always, *always* with fruit pay attention to any rotten spots or blemishes, any soft or squishy patches inside. The microbes already at work will only get worse and spread, causing the flavor to fall way off. Your goal in harvesting and handling produce is to minimize bruising and crushing so that bad spots don't develop. If there are bruises or minor wounds already, isolate those fruits and,

if need be, cut out the defects. That goes for vegetables, too. Berries are especially prone to damage, so if you buy extra berries, go through them one by one rather than pouring large quantities directly into bowls.

As you plant new things in the garden or begin using plants that were already there, learn how each one should be harvested. For leafy vegetables or those with prominent stalks, that means cutting or snapping the leaves or stalks off one by one, from the outside, rather than cutting across the whole plant. Many herbs are snipped at leaf junctures, either high or low. Individual fruits and vegetables must be carefully plucked or cut from branch or vine. Seed packets and plant catalogues usually include some harvesting information.

Use sharp — not dull — knives or scissors to minimize tissue damage, and when you pluck or pick your way through the garden just lay each bit gently in a wide basket, large bowl, or other open container. That way the plant material won't be crowded or crushed and won't collect moisture that could lead to spoilage. Herbs, especially, need plenty of air circulation as you collect and hold them for short-term storage.

Washing fruit and vegetables takes a deft touch. Generally, less is more in terms of cleaning the produce without damaging it. Here are few tips:

- **Leafy vegetables.** Fill a clean sink with water enough to cover the leaves by several inches. Let them soak, then agitate them slightly to dislodge dust and dirt; as you lift the rinsed leaves from the water, you'll see how much dirt falls to the bottom of the sink. From the water they can go into a colander to drain as you do other preparations; or they can be used immediately, still damp.

- **Root crops.** Scrub very gently with a soft brush or wash with a rough cloth. No need to peel if you don't want to, but if you do peel them, rinse off any new dirt that you've generated.

- **Herbs.** The best cleaning is a rain shower. As soon as the sun comes out to dry the droplets, it's time to harvest. If they need a wash, try spraying them and shaking off the moisture.

- **Berries.** Lay berries in a colander or strainer and spray them with water.

- **Larger fruits.** Give fruits like apples and peaches a quick rub in a sink full of water, to knock the dust off. Both organic and conventionally grown citrus may be waxed, so be sure to wash or rub this off before using the zest. Fruits like watermelon don't need such careful cleaning, as you won't be using the rind.

LOTS OF GADGETS are available that can take a bit of the uncomfortable bending and stretching out of the fruit harvest. Some orchard ladders have a tripod base for stability, while others come to a graceful point that fits well into tight branches. Berry rakes and basket pickers make fruit collection faster and easier.

equipment: keeping it simple

A PERSON COULD GO BROKE buying kitchen equipment for processing and preserving homegrown beverages. And, gosh, wouldn't it be fun to have a kitchen full of gadgets! But the truth is, it doesn't take any expensive equipment to have terrific success with juices, fermented beverages, syrups, and teas. The simplest and most economical way to make fruit juices and vegetable drinks involves a lot of boiling and not much else in the way of preparation. That goes for canning, too. In the case of fruit juices there's some straining of solids involved. Here are the basics that you'll need.

Two large stainless-steel bowls. Buy the largest ones you can locate and afford; seriously, you need ones that can hold several gallons of liquid. And you need at least two because one always seems to be filled with fruit and one is always holding some strained juice. There's much ladling of liquids between bowls as you let solids settle out of just-cooked fruit.

Stainless-steel containers provide a non-reactive surface (that is, one that does not react chemically with fruits or juices to spoil the color and taste), and when full of heavy juice they are easier to handle than other nonreactive containers, such as glass or ceramic.

Of course, the more bowls the better, and a variety of sizes is helpful. The nested sets of three are handy. We find ourselves sometimes using as many as six bowls in the course of making a single recipe, especially while washing different produce in batches and preparing ingredients in different ways.

Saucepans and stockpots. You need one nonreactive cooking pot or stockpot that can hold several gallons of boiling liquid. Enameled cast iron is superb, because it can reach high temperatures but also can hold the low temperatures called for in some recipes. Stainless steel is fine, but because the material is thinner than enameled cast iron the contents can scorch more easily. Copper, of course, is lovely, but a big copper pot can cost hundreds of dollars.

A colander, a strainer, cheesecloth, and towels. A large colander for washing fruit makes for easier handling of batches of produce. If you don't have a food mill (see page 39), a large-mesh strainer is a must-have piece of equipment to strain out seeds and pulp, usually through a layer of cheesecloth, coarse muslin, or other food-grade filter cloth. The strainer should sit high enough above your big bowls so that liquid can collect underneath. If the strainer does not sit high enough, pull the corners of the cheesecloth together

to form a bag, and hang the juice bag above the collecting bowl (see photo on the next page). For syrups, use a small fine-mesh strainer.

When straining large quantities of juice we might use up to two yards of cheesecloth per batch. Because it is so gauzy, cheesecloth can't take laundering once you've used it, and the expense can add up if you don't buy in bulk. Although readily available in grocery store baking aisles, the unit cost is high. Many restaurant supply stores and fabric stores sell cheesecloth in large packages. Unbleached muslin

also works well and can take some laundering.

For canning, throw in one or two lightweight cotton kitchen towels or tea towels to wipe the mouths of the jars before they get sealed. You'll need to keep these sanitized by scrupulous laundering. You can also use paper towels, since they are close to sterile.

Ladles, mashers, spoons, and other tools. A large cooking spoon for stirring and a soup ladle, both of stainless steel, will suffice for simple fruit juices. The ladle helps lift clear juice off the

INSTEAD OF USING cheesecloth to hang and strain large quantities of cooked fruit juice, as shown here, head to the paint store or hardware store for a new five-gallon mesh bag designed for straining paint. Run the bag through the dishwasher to sanitize it, or soak it in hot water, hand-wash it, and then rinse it carefully.

solids after straining. A masher of some sort is helpful in various recipes. Other than that, you'll need a paring knife, a chopping knife, and a cutting board. We don't care to use wooden utensils and cutting boards as they discolor and are relatively soft, but there's no harm in doing so.

Canning supplies. If you are going to do canning (rather than freezing or just refrigerator storage), you'll need

USE THE RIGHT JARS

For water-bath or pressure canning you must use heat-tempered canning jars (commonly known as mason jars), which can withstand the rigorous temperature and pressure requirements of home canning. Tempered jars have strong threads where the lids and bands screw on, to help with sealing. Recycled ordinary grocery store jars used for factory-processed foods (mustard, mayonnaise) are cheaper than home-canning jars and not made to withstand repeated stresses.

Today's well-made mason jars will last for many seasons. They can be reused, reheated, and resealed. Mason jars commonly come in sizes from 4 ounces to 64 ounces (half-gallon), and unusual sizes can be ordered online. A box of new mason jars usually costs around $10.

a boiling-water canner, which is a 21-quart or similar size pot with a metal rack inside. Canners are usually made of lighter materials than other large pots because they must be filled with enough water to submerge half a dozen or more quart jars. A cook has to be able to carry the whole shebang from the sink to the stove and back. Canners can be aluminum or enamelware (enamel over aluminum); in this case reactive aluminum is all right because the food never directly touches the surface.

In addition to special jars (see Use the Right Jars), canning requires just a few must-have items: a wide-mouth funnel, canning tongs, and perhaps a magnet

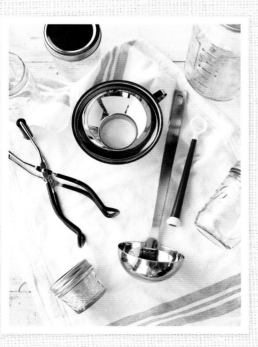

on a stick. The funnel prevents a lot of mess in filling jars; the canning tongs makes it easier to get jars in and out of boiling water; and the magnet, sold alongside canning equipment, makes it easy to fish lids out of scalding water.

Jars come in many sizes and can be sterilized and used over and over. Lids are replaced with every use (but don't cost much), and the bands that hold lids in place must be replaced if they become bent, dented, or rusty.

Syrups typically aren't canned in a water bath, but are poured into sterilized decorative bottles with swing tops (see photo, page 30), so a small funnel is handy to have.

Labeling materials. It doesn't matter what you use, but it is important to label everything you make with a name and date. Listing ingredients is also a good idea. You can use a permanent marker on canning lids, and grease pencils (also called china markers) on bottles of wine, mead, or other fermented beverages.

We find it most convenient to make and print our own labels on the computer and affix them with clear packing tape. The labels stay on but are easy to remove when the jar is empty, and the packing tape keeps them from mildewing if you store them in the basement. Or you can use old-timey heavy paper labels tied on with string for a real homemade look.

more and bigger equipment

Let's say that your first garden beverage efforts were successful, and now you're ready to move up to more production. Here are some upgrades that won't break the bank but that will improve efficiency.

Harvest baskets and containers.
Having a variety of containers for picking and short-term storage makes harvesting and processing easier. For orchard fruits, use a sturdy half-peck or six-quart basket with a comfortable handle; this kind of basket is designed for stability as well as capacity, and you can set one on the ground knowing it won't tip over. Berries crush easily, and they stain, so pick them in small quantities and use small plastic buckets that can be washed. Herbs and flowers retain their shape well if laid onto a wide, shallow basket called a trug. A well-ventilated wire basket or colander lets dirt, dust, and bugs fall away as you gather.

Plastic buckets like five-gallon drywall buckets are a no-no. Moisture collects at the bottom, and the fruit, if left too long, can rot. If you need to pick into a plastic bucket, transfer the fruit to something open at the earliest opportunity, as the weight of the heavy fruit on top can bruise lower layers.

Food scales and measuring buckets.
When you make homegrown beverages, the finished quantities will vary depending on how much you harvest, so there's no such thing as an exact recipe. Instead, you'll often need to measure secondary ingredients according to the

OLD OR NEW?

This is a good time to talk about a tricky subject: whether to advocate getting used (or vintage) equipment to save money and energy. Please keep in mind that the pedigree of something as prosaic as a ceramic crock or cooking pot really matters. If you buy a crock at an auction, you don't know what toxic substance might have touched those inside surfaces. Crocks can last a long time, so this is an important consideration.

Ditto for a cooking pot that might have tiny craters that have held something unsavory at one time. Beware! It's a different matter if you have inherited a grandmother's treasured stewpot that never left the kitchen.

We like the prices for new equipment at restaurant supply stores. Everything at a restaurant supply store is food-grade, large-scale, and economical; advanced machinery and equipment is also available. See if there's such a store near you that's open to the public, or check online. An Asian grocery store is another source for inexpensive large bowls, strainers, and other equipment.

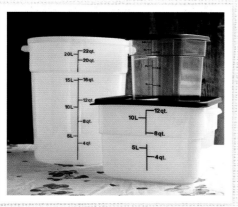

amount of raw juice you have produced. Restaurant supply stores carry food-grade buckets with marks for measuring volume, and they also carry various sizes of scales for calculating weights.

Electric food dehydrator. Wonderful for so many uses, dehydrators are especially good for drying herbs quickly and at the best temperature so that flavors stay fresh. Dehydrators range in cost from about $40 on up. If you are dehydrating large quantities, consider also getting a vacuum sealer and a supply of reusable plastic bags. The equipment may cost around $100, but vacuum-sealing prolongs the shelf life of your ingredients considerably.

By preserving your surplus herbs this way, you can make all sorts of beverages at your own convenience, rather than only at harvesttime. Without an electric dehydrator, you can still dry many herbs to suitable quality, either by hanging them upside down in bunches in a closet or attic, or by laying them in a single layer on a cookie sheet and covering them with cheesecloth to keep

bugs off. *Please* don't dry your herbs in the oven! Ovens can rarely be set to a temperature low enough (about 100°F) to dry herbs without destroying the essential oils.

Immersion blender, food mill. Both these devices will help you produce smoother juice or vegetable drinks. The immersion blender has blades that you can put right into a cooking pot and whir, and it does not grind any seeds present. The cost varies from $40 to more than $100. A food mill is a low-tech version: it looks something like a saucepan with a perforated bottom and a crank handle attached to a bent metal blade; the blade strains the food through the bottom as the handle is turned. A food mill can help you process the seeds out of tomato drinks or berries before you can them. Prices start around $45.

Big canning jars. To make the most of a large apple, pear, or tomato harvest, up-size your canning capacity by using half-gallon rather than quart canning jars, as long as you think you'll drink the full half-gallon in seven to ten days. That's the maximum recommended length for safe refrigeration. For example, a family with children might benefit from the half-gallon jars, while a single person would not.

Generally, all canning supplies are reasonably priced, but you might find some beautiful ways to spend money on decorative gift bottles.

top-of-the-line equipment

There are two big-ticket items that we heartily recommend if you have access to a large supply of fruit or vegetables: a fruit press and a commercial-grade food processor. Both pieces of equipment put you in the major leagues and represent a serious investment of time and money. Consider investing in one or both with a community group, a food cooperative, or your extended family.

Fruit press. Fruit presses operate by means of a ratcheting screw lever to squeeze juice from various orchard fruits; the fruit must first be chopped or ground into chunks before being collected in a slat-sided wooden "basket,"

so a press is often paired with a grinder. Note that a fruit press is not appropriate for stone fruits like peaches or plums, because those pits will break the grinder teeth, but it is perfect for apples, pears, grapes, and other relatively soft fruits. If you want to use a fruit press with stone fruits, the pits must be removed by hand, no matter what the quantity.

The range of prices for a fruit press and grinder is huge, starting at several hundred dollars and increasing to more than a thousand dollars. The disparity represents differences in capacity and materials and whether the press is hand-powered or run by electricity. Power presses, which will give you many times more juice per hour than a hand press, are necessary only for commercial or near-commercial operations. Whatever model you choose, keep in mind that a thorough cleaning after each fruit pressing is part of the process (see Keeping a Press Clean, page 57).

Here's why anyone should consider a fruit press: the juice (with no water added) is extracted by pressure and not by heat and is therefore far superior in

A HAND-OPERATED HARDWOOD FRUIT PRESS can quickly turn five gallons of chopped fruit like apples, grapes, or pears into a gallon or two of spectacular juice. However, a fruit press requires more cleaning and more storage space than stovetop extraction utensils, so it is most suitable for making large volumes or for sharing the work with a group. Shown here is the grinder, set up to process the fruit before it's pressed. See more about using a press starting on page 56.

flavor. There's simply no comparison: juice made by heat extraction is very good, but cold-pressed juice is out of this world.

Commercial-grade food processor.

Costing about $500, a commercial-grade food processor will eventually pay for itself in beverages. It makes short work of chopping or grinding fruit for quick heat extraction, and of combining vegetables and other ingredients in large batches. A commercial-grade food processor is engineered to handle heavy loads; in some cases the motor will shut off temporarily if it heats up and then reset so that you can keep going.

A HEAVY-DUTY APPLIANCE can chop a lot of fruit, such as apples, quickly without burning out the motor.

This tool is also useful in conjunction with a fruit press, if you have a press without a grinder attachment.

Juicers. A third category of big-ticket juice-making equipment is an actual juicer. These come in several electric models, each with its own mechanical characteristics and special strengths for the foods they process: centrifugal juicers, masticating juicers, and triturating (or twin-gear) juicers. Some can be quite loud, some are a bit slow, and not all turn out great quantities of juice for the work. Prices start at just over $100 and go right up to $1,000 or more.

On the plus side, electric juicers can extract nutritious fresh juice from all kinds of produce (except herbs), and these juices might best be consumed by the glass. Frankly, because we learned juice production using lower-tech methods, our experience lies elsewhere.

A stainless-steel steam juicer is not as complicated or expensive as the mechanical juicers, and costs from $100 up. Steam juicers have several basket-like layers and produce juice from soft fruits and vegetables using steam from boiling water; the juice is forced out of the produce and falls back down into a collector pan. The process is generally slower than boiling and straining.

WHAT ABOUT WINEMAKING EQUIPMENT?

Making wine, meads, and other fermented beverages requires just a few pieces of specialized equipment. Here's a list based on our homegrown beverage experience:

FERMENTING EQUIPMENT. It's possible to make excellent wines and meads, even liqueurs, with the very cheapest of equipment, although serious hobbyists eventually start spending more on upgrades. All you need for your first batch is a one-gallon glass jug left over from store-bought cider or purchased for less than $5 at a home brew supply store, a large funnel, and an airlock with a stopper that fits in the mouth of your jug. The airlock allows gas to escape without letting oxygen affect your fermentation.

In addition, as part of the racking process to remove developing wines from the fermentation waste, you will need a four-foot length of ⅜-inch plastic siphon hose to transfer liquid between containers. You will also need such other inexpensive supplies as a racking cane and a bottle brush. For bottling, you will need a five-gallon plastic pail with a tap, or a bottle wand, used with the same siphon hose. You can use recycled wine bottles (though you'll have to buy new corks) or sanitized beer bottles that you can seal with a simple capping device that costs around $20. That's all!

WINEMAKING UPGRADES. After your first few successful batches of wine or mead, you may want to refine your equipment. Actually, the standard one-gallon glass jug is convenient for making small quantities of any wine because it's easy to wash and light enough to carry. But for larger batches you can get three-gallon or five-gallon carboys, which are stout glass vessels with a small neck and mouth. The cost starts around $35. Along with the chunky carboys you'll need big bottle brushes to clean the inside.

Once wine production ramps up you may want to buy, or at least sanitize and recycle, regular 750–milliliter wine bottles with corks, instead of beer bottles with caps. Hand-operated wine-corking mechanisms start at around $30.

Home brew supply stores also sell various devices to measure alcohol content, sugar levels, and so on.

1 gallon carboys

funnels

measuring cup

airlock and stopper

racking hose and cane

bottle brush

clear the decks!

WE GET A TINGLY FEELING when there's something wonderful to harvest plus an interesting recipe for those fresh ingredients. And here's what we do with that tingly feeling before channeling it into chopping, boiling, mixing, and bottling: We clear the decks for a period of assembly-line work. We prepare the kitchen by removing all extraneous items from work surfaces, and assembling and sanitizing all the equipment and materials we need. Your work will be easier if all your kitchen counters are cleared off *and* cleaned before you start.

Sanitation is crucial to the quality of homegrown beverages; therefore, many of our preparation chores center on getting all the equipment clean, but not too early. It doesn't do much good to wash all your equipment for a batch of wine, for example, if it then sits out collecting dust or, worse, spores of airborne yeast or other microbes that could impede proper fermentation.

If you have space, consider isolating specialty gadgets for beverage production in a separate cupboard, closet, or plastic bag. If your implements aren't banging around a drawer with lots of other utensils, they are less likely to pick up bugs that can compromise quality.

Here are our guidelines for preparation:

Do you have enough time? Beverage production can take up a lot of space, and you may not be able to clear away the works to make dinner while in the midst of pressing fruit or canning. Make sure you have blocked out enough time for the entire process of each recipe. Cleaning a fruit press, both before and after production, is a big deal, so make sure to count that time, too.

Our recipes note how much time, exclusive of cleaning, you will need: actual preparation time plus waiting time while liquids settle properly. We find it helpful to schedule harvest and production days, marking them on the calendar so that peak harvest-times don't slip away.

Do you have enough space? Remember all those bowls and pots and stockpots and strainers and jars we mentioned earlier? Once you get going on a recipe you may fill every inch of counter space and sink space, at least for a few minutes at a time. Clear out the dishwasher, clear out the sink, clear off the counters. Then wipe them clean.

Check the refrigerator to make sure there's room to store juice overnight and let solids settle out. It's not a good idea to let juices sit out at room temperature overnight once they have dripped through a strainer; generally the idea is to chill them while the solids settle. Later, if you choose to can your juices, they will be reheated to nearly boiling as part of the canning process.

Finally, figure out beforehand where you will be able to store your finished beverages. Both canned beverages and those undergoing fermentation do best in a dark or semidark place with an even temperature around 65–70°F. If you are freezing beverages, make sure you have your freezer containers at hand and that there's room for them in the freezer.

Wash everything! Even if you think your tools are clean, wash them again before you begin. Best practices, especially pertaining to canning and fermentation, call for you to sterilize all equipment: every spoon, jar, and strainer. We'll give you more details in later chapters on canning and winemaking, but figure on running everything through the dishwasher or washing by hand with soap and very hot water.

For best results, we also recommend that as you finish using each utensil, bowl, or strainer you wash it out immediately and pack it away or at least stack it for convenient reuse. We're not being overly dramatic. If you let things pile up at any time in the production process you can get in a jam. If the sink is full of dirty bowls, you can't use it for pouring hot liquids through a strainer.

All that's left to do is to wash your produce. Because all your bowls and strainers are clean and ready to use, that's a snap.

Now, let's get cooking!

KITCHEN SAFETY

You need to guard against burns, cuts, and scrapes while processing large quantities of fruit. Even in hot weather wear an apron, a long-sleeved shirt, and rubber gloves. Always wear closed-toe shoes, and be sure to tie back long hair. Strictly speaking, all these choices are optional, of course, but we highly recommend them.

juices & fermented beverages

4

creating fruit & vegetable drinks

Orchard fruits, berries, vine fruits, and various fruiting wildflowers make for wonderful drinking. There's practically no limit to what you can turn into beverages. For example, by adding filtered water and yeast you can turn a quart of mulled apple cider left over from Thanksgiving dinner into nearly a gallon of wine that will be ready for holidays a year later. The cost? About $3!

Tomato-based vegetable drinks can be consumed at once or put up to be used alone or as mixers. These wonderful beverages contain plenty of vitamin C and other nutrients, and the goodness quotient goes higher and higher the more leafy vegetables, root crops, and herbs you throw in, as long as you also follow proper canning procedures. Tomatoes, technically, *are* fruits, and we treat them much like the other high-yield crops.

In writing this book, we conducted trial-and-error kitchen experiments to help other gardeners take advantage of their best and biggest crops. We aimed to create recipes realistic enough and clear enough for first-time cooks and canners, yet flexible enough for experienced hands to adapt. Our juice and vegetable drinks are presented in an order that coincides with the growing and harvest season, from about May through October. You'll see at a glance just what crops did well where we live, in the southern Appalachian Mountains. If you have a different selection of local produce available, it should be easy to mix and match your harvest with our recipes.

THE FRUIT JUICE MANIFESTO

We make our own juices so that we can control the contents of the drinks we serve and enjoy. We make our own juices to help lower the energy footprint of our diet. We make our own juices to create countless other exciting beverages and save money on everyday drinks and party drinks, too. Mostly, though, we make our own juices for health, flavor, and freshness.

Yes, grocery-store shelves and refrigerator cases are lined row after row of brightly colored fruit and vegetable juices and drinks. With all that convenience, and no cooking time, why not just drink those? Can it really cost that much less to do it yourself? Can the contents be that much better? For answers, let's read the fine print on some of those grocery-store beverages:

A HOUSE-BRAND 100 PERCENT ORANGE JUICE. The orange juice concentrates are shipped in from Brazil, Mexico, and Costa Rica, and then mixed with concentrates from somewhere in the United States. In comparison, homegrown rose hip tea is fresher, has loads more vitamin C, and involves no transportation costs and less pollution.

A CRANBERRY-GRAPE DRINK. Oops, just 15 percent juice, this pretty beverage is mostly water, with berry juice, cane sugar, and carrot purée, plus various additives.

A "POWER C" VITAMIN DRINK. Many of the contents may actually be right at hand (and super fresh) in your own garden, such as apple, mango, orange, guava, peach, strawberry, rose hip, and a tropical cherry. Get inspired to improvise your own factory-free recipes.

A BERRY-VEGETABLE DRINK. With high carbohydrate levels and four times the minimum daily requirement of vitamin C (the excess is just excreted), this product comes from mixing concentrates and purées, plus nearly a dozen additives. Why not come up with your own homegrown fruit and vegetable drinks, and control the quality of every ingredient yourself?

AND COST? Try $8 a quart — that's right, a quart — for at least one of the grocery-store drinks described above. That means $32 a gallon. Wow. Not that expensive, perhaps, if you buy the organic produce to make these drinks yourself, but when you grow your own, the price per quart goes down year after year as yields increase.

We believe that $100–$200 in onetime expenses for the most straightforward juicing and canning equipment, plus perhaps $30 more for winemaking basics, will pay you back many times over. You'll get gallons and gallons of delicious beverages throughout the years, at a fraction of the grocery store cost. But can we even put a price on the difference?

juice or cider

PLEASE NOTE THAT SOME of our drink recipes are called "juice" and others "cider." We distinguish between the two this way: Drinks made from cooking or steaming fruit to extract the flavorful liquid are *juices*. Those extracted by pressure without any heat are *ciders*. Juice and cider from the same crop, say, apples, taste significantly different and have distinctive handling characteristics. The cider is not diluted with water, so the flavor profile is more intense and the texture more dense with fiber.

Furthermore, because ciders are not subjected to high heat, the wild yeast they contain is still living and can produce delicious hard, or fermented, cider under ideal conditions (see chapter 5). But heat-extracted juices need to have sugar or honey plus live yeast added for any fermentation to occur.

We begin with fruit juices because they form the basis for many of the other recipes later in the book. And they're easy — after you have had success with one kind of fruit juice, you can begin to improvise. We encourage you not only to make pure fruit juices, such as apple or grape or pear, but to mix different fruits into juice combos if they happen to come ripe at the same time. Try crab apple–grape or strawberry-peach or anything else that pleases you.

MAKING FRUIT LEATHERS

After processing juicy, pulpy fruits, such as strawberries and peaches, you may be left with enough flavor-saturated material to make fruit leathers in a dehydrator. Let two cups or so of this leftover pulp sit overnight in a fine-mesh strainer or cheesecloth to reduce excess moisture. Then fill special fruit leather trays with a thin layer of the fruit, and set according to manufacturer's instructions.

Strawberries make bright fruit leather, but peaches may need the addition of a little lemon juice to prevent discoloration.

how to make juice

PRODUCING JUICE FROM FRUIT requires taking some kind of physical action to break open the cells that contain the juice and then straining out skin, seeds, and pulp before bottling or fermenting the filtered juice. In most cases you can strain the initial liquid through a large cheesecloth-lined colander sitting over a bowl. For best results, we usually recommend letting the strained juice sit overnight so that more solids can sink to the bottom, leaving you with the best, clearest juice possible!

For some especially pulpy fruits or with large batches of anything, it may help to make a sling out of cheesecloth or muslin to suspend cooked fruit over the collecting bowl. Figuring out how to suspend the heavy fruit in the sling may be the most difficult part of juice making, so you can see it's not rocket science.

There are two main methods for making juice: extracting it from the fruit with heat or pressing it from the fruit. You can also use a steam extractor if you want to get really serious (see opposite page.

For heat extraction, clean the fruit; chop it if necessary, leaving peels on; put the fruit into a large, heavy cooking pot; and barely cover it with filtered water. Bring to the boil and simmer, stirring and mashing occasionally until the fruit breaks apart and the juice is running freely. Skim off foam as it forms. Turn off the heat and strain the liquid.

Here's the only refinement: If the fruit is already small or soft, as in the case of berries and grapes, there's no need to cut it before cooking; the skins will break apart with the heat (except for very thick-skinned grape varieties). Orchard fruits must be cut into pieces, either by hand or in a heavy-duty food processor or blender, depending on quantity. Otherwise, you will lose some of the flavor because not enough surface area is exposed and the cooking process just can't do it all. An immersion blender at this stage can help liberate more juice from thick fruit skins and pulp during cooking by grinding up the cooking fruit in the stock pot.

Stovetop heat extraction is economical and foolproof. We don't recommend doing it with young children nearby or pets underfoot, but you can start and

STEAM EXTRACTION: QUITE THE PROCESS

Rather than boiling fruit in water to extract juice, a stainless-steel steam extraction setup, a big contraption, uses steam to break down the cell walls and release the juice. The juice runs downward as steam cooking goes on and is collected in the middle chamber of the extractor, and then can be siphoned into canning jars.

Steam extractors are a bit complicated, consisting of three large sections plus a lid and some piping. People like steam extractors for several reasons. The concentrated juice is superb in quality, rich in flavor and color, and clear without extra filtering. Because the juice comes from the extractor so hot, it can be directed into sterilized canning jars without the further processing needed for vacuum sealing in water-bath canning. Voilà!

There are other considerations, though. The steam extractor is quite bulky and comes in several pieces, so not only do you need room to store it, but every piece must be carefully washed each time before storage.

In contrast, regular stovetop extraction just uses a big pot. Some chopping of larger fruit is necessary with the steam extractor.

Steam extractors need to be carefully monitored during the entire process so that the boiling-water pan that creates the steam doesn't go dry, and that can be as long as 90 minutes. The steam and all the parts get extremely hot, and handling the siphon hose from the collection chamber to the hot canning jars can be tricky. Young children must not be allowed in the area.

Keep in mind, too, that the yield in one batch of steam-extracted juice maxes out at about one gallon. If you have a huge crop, this may not be the right tool because of the processing and cleanup times required.

Frankly, we didn't include a steam extractor on any of our equipment lists because we have always found the stovetop method safer and easier.

stop the process easily if you need to leave the room. This method is ideal for processing small quantities of fruit, say, four quarts at a time, and can easily be upsized to handle large amounts.

using a food processor

We previously mentioned using an industrial-strength food processor or blender in connection with stovetop heat extraction (see page 42). In our experience, it takes a heavy-duty appliance to chop a lot of fruit quickly without burning out the motor. Remember to remove the pits from stone fruits (peaches, apricots, plums) before putting them in a food processor or blender.

stovetop heat extraction

1. The first step is to clean and chop all your fruit into halves or quarters, removing bruises and other bad spots. You can leave apple or pear seeds, but remove the pits from stone fruits. Don't peel the fruit — you don't want to lose any flavor!

2. Put the fruit in a large heavy stockpot and barely cover it with filtered water. Bring to the boil and simmer, stirring and mashing occasionally until the fruit breaks apart and the juice is running freely. The amount of time will depend on the type of fruit you are processing.

3. After the fruit has begun to soften, a stick blender comes in very handy for breaking up the pieces and releasing more juice as the fruit cooks. If you don't have an immersion blender, you can use a food processor or blender, working in batches. Handle the hot liquid carefully!

4. As the fruit cooks, foam will form on the surface of the juice. Skim off foam with a large spoon several times during the cooking process. Turn off the heat and let the juice cool for a while before handling it.

5. Set a large colander over a clean stockpot and line it with two layers of cheesecloth or muslin dampened with filtered water. Pour the juice into the colander. (You can use a large glass measuring cup to transfer the first of the juice.) Let the juice sit at room temperature for the time recommended in the recipe.

6. Another method of straining is to gather the corners of the fabric into a strong knot and hang the resulting bag over the collection vessel (we usually tie it to a cabinet knob). With either method, it's tempting to squeeze the pulp to extract a few final drops of juice, but **don't!** You'll just make your juice cloudy or pulpy.

THE FRUIT THAT IS LEFT after pressing is called pomace. It can be cooked into juice to increase your yield from one harvest. See Happy Time Pear Juice, page 88.

using a fruit press

Having discussed fruit presses briefly in chapter 3, now is the time for some honest talk about life with one. The highest highs and the lowest lows belong to this humble piece of equipment. The juice is the best you can make. Period. It's what we are calling cider, and when you have finished drinking a season's supply, probably too quickly, you will dream about that ambrosia all winter.

But a fruit press requires more maintenance, in the form of frequent deep cleaning, than any other device for making juice. Is a press worth the expense and bother? You be the judge. For starters, you'll need a clean, dry storage area for the off-season, and you should cover the main parts with plastic bags to guard against dust and mold. The presence of any microbes can affect the quality of beverages.

The fruit press we use consists of a panlike enameled metal base on legs, screwed to a square of wood for stability; the base has a lip that allows liquid to run off, and a huge upright screw anchored in the middle. An open wood basket sits on top of the base, and once it is filled with fruit, up to five gallons at a time, we cover the top with special wooden plates. The lever assembly fits over the big screw and tightens against the plates. The cider runs out the bottom into a collection bowl.

We have found that any fruit press activity takes at least half a day. Realistically, four hours gives you time to set up, sterilize, wash and chop fruit, press, and clean up. And because a fruit press can produce several gallons of cider at one time, you need to clear out your refrigerator or other cool-storage space to store the cider until it can be processed by canning, freezing, or fermenting; maximum time to store unprocessed cider in the refrigerator is about a week.

The heavy workload and the steep price of a fruit press make it a good candidate for group ownership: an extended family, a food co-op, or a neighborhood association. One warning: In the event of group ownership, to share the work *and* the fun of pressing, someone has to be responsible for cleaning the parts correctly. The moment the press starts to build up sugar residues on parts, the quality of your pressings can suffer.

An alternative to ownership by a large group would be ownership by an intimate cooking club or winemaking club. Such an arrangement also makes good use of big bowls, strainers, and other equipment that the members can share.

KEEPING A PRESS CLEAN

Here's the cleaning regimen for a typical home fruit press: Before you press fruit, you will need to take the parts out of storage, wash them or wipe them down, and pour scalding water over each part to sterilize the surfaces. That step really helps if you are planning to make mead or wine with your cider.

Once you have finished crushing the fruit in the basket, there will be pulp and seeds oozing over all the parts, plus insects attracted to the sugar bonanza, and now the basket must be hosed off, then washed and thoroughly rinsed and dried. The metal lever and ratchet mechanism needs even stricter care; the parts must be washed and completely dried, and then oiled with olive oil or other food-grade lubricant and packed into plastic bags.

Then there's the grinder attachment, which makes quick work of big fruits like apples and pears, and gets them ready to press in a few minutes. But the grinder, especially, needs before-and-after sterilization. Its many sharp surfaces can trap sugars that foster the growth of stray organisms over long storage periods.

1. Chop the fruit into halves or quarters depending on the size. Cut crab apples in half. As a rough guide, a bushel of apples will produce about a gallon of cider.

2. One person feeds the fruit into the hopper of the grinder while the other cranks the blades. This process breaks the fruit down further and makes it easier to press, as well as helping to release more cider. Grinding a bushel of apples into a large container doesn't take long – about 30 minutes.

3. The ground fruit is loaded into the press. Once the press is full, the pressing plates go in place. You may have to press in batches, depending on the size of your press and the quantity of fruit you are processing. A bushel of apples may require two batches.

4. The pressing blocks come between the handle and ratchet to give extra pressing power.

5. As the handle works the mechanism, the plates move downward to extract the cider. Additional blocks are added as the plates go lower. The farther down the plates move, the harder it is to work the handle — pressing cider can be quite a workout!

6. Collect the juice in bowls or other large containers and then transfer it into bottles and jugs as needed for processing.

Making cider is a sticky process so wear old clothes.

refrigeration and freezing

REFRIGERATION IS FOR SHORT-TERM storage only, with research suggesting periods of less than a week for keeping fresh fruit juices in the refrigerator. If you have a large volume of fresh juice to preserve over a period of time, we suggest that you can or ferment it rather than trying to refrigerate it.

The refrigerator *is* a good place to store juices during processing, or to store unsealed or already opened jars of juice. Keeping juice out overnight on a counter is a very bad idea, since the safe temperatures for refrigeration range between 40°F and 32°F. Watching the temperature of your juices once they are done cooking is crucial because bacteria can grow rapidly in temperatures above 40°F, affecting the quality of your products.

We find that most of the juice from a batch of cooked fruit will drip through cheesecloth or another filter in an hour or so. More may drip out later, but after the first hour refrigerate what you have collected. Let the rest drip out for a few more hours, and then combine everything and refrigerate until further processing.

freezing is a fine option

Rapid freezing is perhaps the most effective method for preserving the nutrition, color, and flavor of freshly picked foods. That's because a deep freeze stops bacterial action and prevents spoilage. Freezing is also attractive because juices can be kept safely for up to a year, and the technique works well with small batches of juice. And in a hot summer kitchen, freezing juices is more comfortable than canning, which requires additional boiling water.

The big downside of freezing is that if electric power goes off for more than a few hours, you risk losing an entire harvest. While freezing offers many good features, perhaps you shouldn't make it your only method of preserving the harvest. And by all means, "rotate your stock" by checking dates to make sure juice hasn't outlived its freezer life of six months to a year. In the event of a power failure, it is permissible to re-freeze thawed juice as long as it stays fairly cold, but the quality of the product suffers because of separation and flavor deterioration. Just don't bother.

Several safeguards apply if you do freeze juice.

Cool juices quickly. Once you have made your juice, cool it quickly by setting the bowl of juice in a larger bowl containing ice.

Use high-quality freezer containers. Do not use glass jars for freezing juice, unless you have tapered wide-mouth jars and leave plenty of headspace for expansion. Even so, tempered glass jars can become brittle when going from freezing temperatures to room

temperature, and we don't like the danger of glass shards.

For best results, use high-quality plastic freezer containers with snap-on lids. A quart or half-gallon size works well for juices. Larger sizes can be too bulky and slow to thaw. To prevent any large ice crystals forming at the top of the juice (in the headspace), lay a piece of heavy plastic wrap directly onto the surface of the juice before snapping on the lid and freezing.

Another method that works well is to freeze the juice in ice cube trays for 24 hours and then transfer the frozen cubes into high-quality freezer bags. This makes it easy to take the exact amount of juice you want from the freezer without wasting any. Plus, who doesn't like fruit-flavored ice cubes in their drinks?

Add ascorbic acid. Frozen juices can oxidize, turning a bit brown as they thaw, so we recommend you use a teaspoon of ascorbic acid (vitamin C) or six crushed 500-milligram vitamin C tablets per each gallon of juice before freezing. In addition, you may want to add a bit of sugar to your juices if you plan to freeze them, to enhance flavor and color.

Label freezer containers. Just as with canned juices, meads, or wines, frozen juices need to be labeled. Using a permanent marker, label each freezer container with the freeze date and contents. It's important not to guess about dates when you need to check the freshness of stock.

Check the temperature. Frozen foods stay safe and appealing only when they are kept at 0°F or below, so use a thermometer to check the temperature in your freezer. Do not overload the freezer, or the temperature can go up.

WHAT'S ASCORBIC ACID?

Ascorbic acid is a form of vitamin C found in almost any canned food at the grocery store, where it is used as a minor ingredient for freshness. You can buy ascorbic acid in the canning section of the grocery store, although it often has dextrose added. Or you can often find pure ascorbic acid at a pharmacy or health food store.

You can feel confident that ascorbic acid is safe. While strictly speaking it is optional, we have found that it really keeps the colors from fading to an unattractive brown and it preserves the fresh taste of the juice very well. In the recipes in this book, we don't list ascorbic acid as optional.

how to can

THE BASICS OF CANNING are extremely easy, and the process is safe. Canning fruit juices and tomato-based vegetable juices involves two stages, and they both take place on the stovetop.

The first stage is heating high-acid liquids nearly to the boiling point, then pouring them into hot, sterilized tempered glass jars or mason jars. (It's a bit confusing, but mason jars, though patented in 1858 by inventor John L. Mason, are most often sold under the brand name Kerr or Ball.) Cap the jars with sterile two-piece jar lids.

In the second stage, the filled jars go into in a boiling-water bath for a specified time. When they come out, the lids vacuum-seal while the contents cool, so harmful microorganisms can't grow inside. Presto! Each lid makes a satisfying *fffp!* when the seal forms.

Of course there are some specific techniques to make the process go

of ingredients going into canned juices determines the quality of the juice when you eventually open the jars.

smoothly, and we'll get to those in a moment. First, let's address the safety concerns that seem to linger about canning, especially among cooks who didn't grow up with home canning.

Canning developed in the early 1800s, mainly as a way to transport large quantities of preserved food to troops during wartime. Although canning was first devised for glass jars and bottles, metal cans were more practical for transportation. Ironically, some of the early cans themselves contained deadly levels of lead. Eventually, however, canning in glass jars became a cheap, practical way to preserve food at home.

Homemakers everywhere began using tempered glass jars to preserve their fruits and vegetables. There are certain guidelines to follow in order to avoid food poisoning. Botulism, a soil-borne pathogen, lives in airless and low-acid environments. Vegetables are low-acid foods, and they must be processed at high temperatures for safety, which requires a pressure canner. However,

we're not talking about that kind of canning in this book, and we don't include any such recipes.

Canning high-acid fruit and tomato-based juices requires only boiling temperature to be safe. (Some tomatoes can be borderline low acid, but our recipes add lemon juice or ascorbic acid to increase acidity, and we talk about that in more detail on page 67.)

Four different classes of ubiquitous microbes (enzymes, molds, yeasts, and bacteria) can affect food but are destroyed at the boiling point of 212°F in high-acid juices:

- **Enzymes** begin turning fruit mushy and unappealing once it has been picked; refrigeration slows enzyme action, and sufficient heat stops it.

- **Molds,** which can also be killed with high heat, grow into fuzzy layers on food; that's the stuff we throw out when we clean the fridge.

- **Yeasts** can cause food to ferment, and these are also killed by high enough heat.

- **Bacteria** take the most heat to kill, and some of the potentially dangerous ones, the ones that live in low-acid foods, do require the 240°F internal temperature of a pressure canner. But such bacteria can't live as well in a high-acid environment like fruit juice.

GLASS-TOP STOVE WARNING

Unfortunately, it may not be safe to use a smooth-top stove for canning. There may not be a burner surface large enough to accommodate the entire canning pot, and even if there is, dents or warping in the pot may prevent adequate contact with the heating surface.

With some models, the heat generated by the boiling-water bath may trip an automatic shutoff before the processing time is complete. Worse, the heat from the pot can actually crack or otherwise damage the cooking surface.

If you have one of these stoves, check manufacturer's instructions about canning. Gas or electric-coil stoves do not have these issues.

ADJUSTING FOR ALTITUDE

At elevations above 1,000 feet it is crucial to increase boiling time, because water boils at a lower temperature in thinner air. The standard adjustments are these:

— Between 1,000 and 3,000 feet, add 5 minutes to the stated processing time.

— Between 3,000 and 6,000 feet, add 10 minutes.

— Between 6,000 and 8,000 feet, add 15 minutes.

— Over 8,000 feet, add 20 minutes.

step-by-step canning

THE MOST IMPORTANT FACTOR of the canning process is to have all components at the same high temperature before you begin. Jars, lids and bands, implements like funnels and tongs, the juice itself, and the water bath should all be scalding; that is, just below the boiling point, or around 190°F. That way you maintain sanitary conditions and, just as important, avoid cracking jars with thermal shock.

Once your juice has been refrigerated overnight to clarify, ladle the clear liquid into a saucepan and reheat it to 190°F for five minutes as you wash and scald the jars, and scald all other equipment. We recommend that you scald jars in the hot-water bath, but heat lids separately in a saucepan of water for 10 minutes without boiling them. Heated lids provide a better seal but boiling them can damage the rubber ring. If you use lids that come with separate rubber rings, those rings also need to be heated.

A canning pot comes with a low rack that fits into the vessel and sits on the bottom, and you should always have the rack in place for scalding the jars. You can scald empty jars in the same water you use for sealing the full ones. Use a set of large canning tongs (sometimes called a jar lifter) to grasp each jar by

the neck and tip out the hot water. Some people find it more convenient to sterilize jars (but, again, not the lids) in the dishwasher; just make sure to run the whole wash-and-dry cycle on hot, and keep the dishwasher closed until you need the jars.

filling the jars

Have a stainless steel soup ladle or other implement ready to transfer hot juice to each jar. If you don't feel comfortable transferring hot liquid with a ladle, use a Pyrex measuring cup with a 2- or 4-cup capacity. A wide-mouth funnel makes the job much neater. Remember, anything that touches the juice must be sterilized and scalding hot. Be sure to leave the proper headspace between the liquid and the rim of the jar. For most juices, that will be ¼ inch, but check the headspace specified in each recipe. The headspace provides a cushion of air that creates the vacuum seal as jars cool after the boiling-water bath.

Before applying a lid and band, wipe the rim of each jar with a clean tea towel or paper towel. By removing any bits of fruit pulp or drops of liquid, you give the lid a uniform surface to produce a good seal. Use a magnetic lid lifter or a small pair of sanitized tongs to lift each lid out of the saucepan of scalding water.

applying the lids

After placing a lid on the jar, screw on a band, *but not too tight*. The role of the band is to gently hold the jar lid in place during the boiling-water bath, and over-tightening can interfere with proper sealing. You will remove the bands after the jars have sealed and cooled, but keep them to use again once you've broken the seal and are storing the jar in the refrigerator.

Only fill as many jars as will fit in the boiling-water bath at one time. A standard canning pot will hold up to seven quarts. Keep the rest of the juice warm, and bring it back to scalding before filling the next batch of jars.

boiling-water bath

As you fill the jars, put each one in the water bath as soon as the lid is in place. If you hold the first few on the counter until they are all full, they might cool too much. You can under-process the juice but you can't really overcook it. In either case, keep the water bath in the canning pot just below the boiling point. The bath should be filled to a level that will cover the full jars by one to two inches.

When all the jars are loaded, cover the bath and bring the water to a full rolling boil. Start your timer then. Processing time depends on the recipe but typically is between 15 and 25 minutes.

We processed such large quantities of juice during the recipe-testing phase of this book that we used an outdoor 40,000 Btu propane cooker (Cajun Cooker) and a 30-quart turkey pot with

BAKING PAN PRECAUTION

In the rare event that a jar cracks or breaks while you're filling it, you'll have a big mess to clean up. To prevent major spills, put a large rimmed cookie sheet or pan on the countertop and place the jars in the pan to fill them. Cleaning up the spills is a snap, because the pan will contain any mess.

REUSING LIDS AND BANDS?

Specialized canning lids and bands come in "regular" and "wide-mouth" sizes to match different size jars. The lids must be replaced after every use: Once a lid has been opened, the thin rubber seal around the edge is no longer safe for canning. The bands may be reused for canning as long as they are in good shape, with no rust or dents.

a basket insert for our canning. This allowed us to process up to 11 quarts of juice at one time. Also, using a basket instead of tongs made it simple to put the jars into the hot water and to take them out.

proper cooling method

While the jars are bubbling away in the boiling-water bath, prepare a place to put them during the cooling phase. Putting hot canning jars directly on a cool counter is not a good idea. Be especially careful if you have marble or other stone countertops!

Jar manufacturers typically recommend placing the jars on a folded dish towel, or you can use a wooden bread board. Lift the jars carefully out of the water with the canning tongs and leave some room among the jars wherever you set them. You can also lift the entire rack out of the canning pot with all the jars in it and set that on a towel or board. Either way, the idea is to handle the hot jars as little as possible to reduce the risk of breakage.

The jars need to cool uniformly and gradually for 12 to 24 hours, depending on their size, before you move them to storage. As they cool, sometimes within a minute of coming out of the water bath and sometimes after several minutes, the jars will make a sweet little popping or sucking sound as they seal. The seal will also pull the lid down tight, and you'll be able to feel that there's no give in the lid. When all the jars are cool enough to handle comfortably, remove all the bands, as manufacturers recommend, saving them for reuse. Once the vacuum seal has formed, the band doesn't do anything and can cause moisture buildup.

safety first!

Any lids that have not sealed will need further attention. You can either keep an unsealed jar of juice in the refrigerator and drink it in the next week, or you can start over within the first 24 hours with reprocessing the jar. In that case you must sterilize a new jar and heat the juice and all the other parts. Unless you have a lot of jars that didn't seal, it usually isn't worth the trouble to reseal.

If your juices appear abnormal in any way after they have been stored for a while, throw them out, jar and all. Signs of trouble are bulging lids, spurting liquid when you open the jar, lack of a popping sound when the jar is opened, "off" odors, or any fuzz or mold on the surface of the juice. We say: If it doesn't look right, don't take chances.

After decades of safe and successful canning — and feeding our families this way — we have come to believe that too many people are too frightened of potential canning mishaps. Just follow instructions. Warnings are there for a purpose, so pay attention to anything that seems wrong.

labeling and storing

Make a practice of labeling every jar with, at minimum, all the contents and the day the jar was processed. Lots of juices tend to look alike, so it's good to know whether you're pulling out Sensational-7 Vegetable Drink or DeNeice's Super-Heated Bloody Mary Mixer, or a jar of Big Wow Grape Cider that looks a lot like Crab Apple Juice.

The date is important because canned juices have a shelf life that you should respect: one to two years. The first year or so, color remains bright. In the second year juices will still be safe to drink, as long as the seal is intact, but the color may be starting to fade and there is likely to be more sediment sitting on the bottom of the jar.

The best place to store jars is in a closed cupboard, at a consistent temperature between 40°F and 70°F. Temperature changes and extremes can shorten shelf life, and light speeds the deterioration of the contents.

Don't leave canned juices on a sunny shelf. A damp basement is also no good; it's best to keep jars dry so that mold and mildew don't grow on the lids.

CHECK THE RECIPE NOTES

The canning process does not vary in method. The only variables are time (depending on size of jars and the nature of the ingredients) and altitude, so check individual recipes for details. Most of our recipes fall within a narrow range of canning times, because of high acid content and all-liquid ingredients, but other recipes vary substantially. Be aware!

TOMATOES AND ACID

We include tomato-based beverages among the high-acid products that are safe to process without a pressure canner. And they are. But as noted earlier in this chapter (page 63), some tomato varieties can be borderline low acid; therefore we advise adding some bottled lemon juice to each jar of canned tomato product.

Tomato science has changed a bit, and while most tomatoes on their own have high enough acidity (that's a pH of 4.6, if you're into chemistry), some of the newer hybrids that are marketed as "very sweet" don't have quite enough acidity alone. Since lemon juice is even more acidic than tomatoes, the standard practice in canning is to add two tablespoons of bottled lemon juice to each quart jar as you fill it with tomato juice. (Why bottled lemon juice? Because it has a standardized degree of acidity, while fresh lemons, like other fresh fruit, may vary substantially with regard to their acid content.)

Besides adding lemon juice to pure tomato juice, it's important to always acidify the tomato-based vegetable drinks. That's because they contain some low-acid ingredients, and our juice recipes Sensational-7 Vegetable Drink and DeNeice's Super-Heated Bloody Mary Mixer will require increased acidity.

1

2

3

4

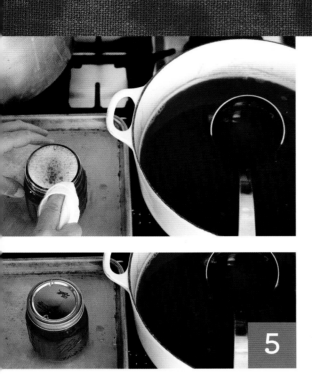

1. Start by sterilizing empty jars in your canning pot, shown here with rack in place. The rack keeps the jars off the direct heat source, reducing the chance of breakage. Hold the jars in scalding water for at least 10 minutes. Heat the lids separately in hot but not boiling water.

2. Heat the juice to 190°F while you are sterilizing the jars. The juice will foam up a bit, but don't worry, that will subside. You can skim the foam off if you want.

3. Remove sterilized jars with canning tongs, draining out as much water as possible. To avoid thermal shock and broken jars, take them out one at a time to fill them.

4. Sterilize the ladle and funnel before using them. Fill each jar with hot juice, leaving the proper headspace, typically a ¼ inch, but check the recipe to be sure.

5. Wipe the rim of the jar with a clean towel before applying the lid and band. Screw on the band lightly to hold the lid in place, and move on to the next jar.

6. Process the jars in the boiling-water bath for the time specified in the recipe, remove the jars from the water, then allow them to cool gradually and completely — 12 to 24 hours — before storing them.

TROUBLESHOOTING GUIDE FOR CANNING

If you are an experienced canner, making and canning juices is easier than making jam or jelly, since there are fewer ways to fail. If you are just beginning, it's easy to succeed from the very first try. Every once in a while, however, you may encounter difficulties, so we'd like to share some of the more common signs of trouble and how to correct them.

LID DOESN'T SEAL OR COMES UNSEALED
Often the fault lies in the rim of the jar: Check for any nicks or chips, as these can affect the sealing process. If a jar has a damaged rim, throw it out. Another fault may be that the rim was not wiped completely clean before the lid was applied. To assure a proper seal, heat the jar lids (but not all the way to boiling) before applying them. And remember, overtightening the bands can interfere with making a proper seal.

Incorrect headspace can also cause seals to fail. Too little headspace can cause beverages to leak out during processing, and juice residue on the lid can prevent proper sealing. Too much headspace can prevent proper sealing because the contents may not have been thoroughly heated.

JARS BREAK DURING CANNING BATH
The fault can be jars with hairline cracks, which may develop after years of use. Regular food jars from the grocery store can easily break, since they are not meant to be heated over and over; the solution is to use only mason jars.

Are you using a rack in the canning water bath? A rack keeps jars from resting directly on the hot surface of the canner and permits the boiling water to circulate completely around the jars for uniform heating.

Thermal shock is a major reason jars break: There is too great a difference between the temperature of the jars and the temperature of their contents, or jars are placed into fully boiling water instead of into hot water. The temperature of all of the items in the canning process (juice, jars, lids, water) must be raised or lowered gradually and in unison. Don't put cold liquid into hot jars or vice versa!

SEDIMENT FALLS TO THE BOTTOM OF THE JAR Several factors can cause sediment to settle gradually on the bottom of jars containing fruit juices. We recommend always using filtered water to make fruit juices with the stovetop heat extraction method. Filtered water minimizes mineral content, which means that flavors will be truer and there is less sediment to settle out.

Depending on the fruit, there may be quite a lot of solids still suspended in the liquid after you have first strained it. That's why we always recommend letting fruit juices sit overnight in a refrigerator before going ahead with canning. You can ladle off the clear juice and strain it again, if you like, to remove even more solids. Grape juice in particular has a lot of sediment.

fruit and vegetable drinks

berry juice

INGREDIENTS

1 flat (12 pints) berries (about 8 pounds), rinsed and picked over

Filtered water, enough to cover berries

Ascorbic acid, ¼ teaspoon per quart of juice (for canning)

Sugar, 2–4 tablespoons per quart of juice (optional, for canning)

BERRY JUICE IS THICK AND DELICIOUS.
This recipe works well with blackberries, raspberries, gooseberries, blueberries, serviceberries, currants, and other ripe berries, either alone or in combination. Use Berry Juice as a pure juice drink or in a smoothie, as a flavor base for carbonated beverages, as a mixer for alcoholic drinks, as a topping for ice cream or other desserts, as a main ingredient in ices and frozen treats, as a milk substitute with cereal, or as an ingredient in baking recipes (to color icing, for instance).

Berry Juice is also a super health drink with cancer-fighting properties in addition to vitamin C and various trace elements, dietary fiber, and compounds that boost heart health, all bound up in a gorgeous package. To keep the flavor lively and the color true, add both ascorbic acid and a little sugar during the canning process.

Although berries can stain clothes and kitchen towels, they are otherwise easy to work with because of their small size and relatively clean growth habit off the ground.

Makes approximately 4 quarts

PREP TIME: About 2 hours, plus overnight for juice to settle, plus canning

1. Put the berries into a large nonreactive stockpot, and then add filtered water to barely cover the fruit. Bring the contents to a boil.

2. Reduce the heat and simmer for 10 minutes, stirring and mashing the berries as they cook, or use an immersion blender to grind the berries. Stir occasionally to avoid sticking, and skim off any foam.

3. Line a large colander with two layers of cheesecloth dampened with filtered water. Set the colander over a large bowl, making sure that the colander sits well above the bottom of the bowl so that the juice can flow freely.

4. Slowly pour the hot berries into the colander.

5. Leave the juice to strain for at least 1 hour. Do not squeeze or force the berries through the cheesecloth, or the juice will become cloudy.

6. Refrigerate the juice overnight in a clean covered container to let solids settle to the bottom. The juice will clear. For canning, ladle the juice out and discard the solids.

This juice can be used immediately or preserved by canning.

strawberry juice

mixed berry juice

Cook's Tip

**You can make this
recipe without the
added sugar, but
the flavor tends to
be flat. Experiment
to find the level
of sweetener that
best suits your
tastes and your
family's needs.**

CANNING NOTES

- Measure the juice by carefully ladling it off the sediments. Pour the measured juice into a nonreactive stockpot.

- Simmer juice at 190°F for 5 minutes. Remove from heat.

- Add sugar, if using (2–4 tablespoons per quart), and stir to dissolve.

- Add ascorbic acid to sterilized jars (¼ teaspoon per quart).

- Fill the jars with liquid, leaving ¼ inch of headspace. Apply sterilized lids and bands, being careful not to over-tighten. Process both pint and quart jars in boiling-water bath for 15 minutes, adjusting for altitude (page 63).

strawberry juice

STRAWBERRY JUICE makes a special treat because the flavor takes an unexpected turn when the berries cook. They lose their cloying sweetness and become a subtle and satisfying drink or mixer. Kids and adults alike enjoy this bright crimson juice. The flavor is actually a little tart, like cherry juice.

There's so much liquid inside fresh strawberries that converting the berries to juice doesn't take as long as with other fruit.

To keep the color bright and the flavor lively, be sure to add ascorbic acid and a little sugar during the canning process.

After the juice has been canned in a boiling-water bath, it really pops, and the flavor is wonderful. It thickens slightly into a lovely, jewel-like liquid that is best diluted in a glass with ice and club soda or water.

Makes approximately 3 quarts

PREP TIME: About 2 hours, plus canning

INGREDIENTS

4 quarts fresh strawberries (8–10 pounds), hulled

Filtered water

Ascorbic acid, ¼ teaspoon per quart of juice (for canning)

Sugar, 2–4 tablespoons per quart of juice (optional, for canning)

1. **Put the strawberries** into a large nonreactive stockpot, and then add filtered water to barely cover the fruit. Bring the contents to a boil.

2. **Reduce the heat** and simmer for 10 minutes, stirring and mashing or blending the berries as they cook. Stir occasionally to avoid sticking, and skim off any foam.

3. **Line a large** colander with two layers of cheesecloth that have been dampened with filtered water. Set the colander over a large bowl, making sure that the colander sits well above the bottom of the bowl so the juice can flow freely.

4. **Slowly pour the** hot strawberry liquid into the cheesecloth-lined colander.

5. **Let the juice** strain for at least 1 hour. Do not squeeze or force the strawberries through the cheesecloth, or the juice will become cloudy.

This juice can be used immediately or preserved by canning.

CANNING NOTES

- Measure the juice by carefully ladling it off any sediments. Pour the measured juice into a nonreactive stockpot.

- Simmer juice at 190°F for 5 minutes. Remove from heat.

- Add sugar, if using (2–4 tablespoons per quart), and stir to dissolve.

- Add ascorbic acid to sterilized jars (¼ teaspoon per quart).

- Fill the jars with liquid, leaving ¼ inch of headspace. Apply sterilized lids and bands, being careful not to overtighten. Process both pint and quart jars in boiling-water bath for 15 minutes, adjusting for altitude (page 63).

Cook's Tip

If you're drinking this juice fresh and you want to add sweetness, either reheat the juice and add sugar to the whole amount, or stir a little sugar into each glass.

peach juice

INGREDIENTS

12–15 pounds of peaches* (about 25–30 medium-sized peaches), cut in half and pitted

Filtered water

Ascorbic acid, ¼ teaspoon per quart of juice (for canning)

Sugar, 4 tablespoons (¼ cup) per quart of juice (optional, for canning)

NOTHING BEATS A FRESH PEACH, and we don't pretend that our Peach Juice comes close to that flavor sensation. But you can capture some of summer's enjoyment for the whole year when you make this beverage from the ripe local harvest. Peach Juice works well as a mixer with other fruit juices, too.

More important, Peach Juice can be used to extend richer juices like blackberry or blueberry, stretching the berry yield. Peach Juice by itself, while good, doesn't have the pizzazz of Berry Juice, but the available quantities are often so much greater.

Be sure to use only perfectly ripe, unblemished fruit for this juice. It may be necessary to cut out some spots, but you can nibble on those overripe bits as you work, or sprinkle them on top of ice cream and drizzle with chocolate sauce for a quick treat.

IMPORTANT: Processed peaches tend to darken once they are exposed to oxygen, and the flavor can change. So it is imperative to add ascorbic acid during the canning process to stop any discoloration and deterioration in flavor.

Makes approximately 4 quarts

PREP TIME: About 2 hours, plus overnight for juice to settle, plus canning

*Any quantity over 10 pounds works well.

1. Put the peaches into a large nonreactive stockpot, and then add filtered water to barely cover the fruit. Bring the contents to a boil.

2. Reduce the heat and simmer for 10 minutes, stirring and mashing or blending the peaches as they cook. Stir occasionally to avoid sticking, and skim off any foam.

3. Line a large colander with two layers of cheesecloth that have been dampened with filtered water. Set the colander over a large bowl, making sure that the colander sits well above the bottom of the bowl so that the juice can flow freely.

4. Slowly pour the hot peaches into the colander. Be careful not to splash the hot liquid.

5. Leave the juice to strain for 24 hours. Do not squeeze or force the peaches through the cheesecloth, or the juice will contain extra pulp.

6. Refrigerate the juice overnight to let solids settle to the bottom. The juice will clear somewhat, but it remains slightly cloudy due to the pectin haze that forms (see Pectin, page 110).

This juice can be used immediately or preserved by canning.

CANNING NOTES

- Measure the juice by carefully ladling it off the sediments. Pour the measured juice into a nonreactive stockpot.

- Simmer juice at 190°F for 5 minutes. Remove from heat.

- Add sugar, if using (2–4 tablespoons per quart), and stir to dissolve.

- Add ascorbic acid to sterilized jars (¼ teaspoon per quart).

- Fill the jars with liquid, leaving ¼ inch of headspace. Apply sterilized lids and bands, being careful not to overtighten. Process both pint and quart jars in boiling-water bath for 15 minutes, adjusting for altitude (page 63).

Cook's Tip

See Peach-Rosemary Syrup, page 187, for a way to turn Peach Juice into something spectacular and surprising. Or try some mulled Peach Juice!

big wow grape cider

GRAPES ARE THE GREATEST! They grow naturally all over North America, from the cool, moist vineyards of upstate New York to the dry volcanic hillsides of northern California, and even in the scorching plains of Oklahoma. Use wild grapes or hybrids, and get ready to taste some of the most complex and exciting flavors in the fruit kingdom. We used fat, sweet, juicy North Carolina muscadine grapes for this recipe.

All ciders are extracted cold with a fruit press, rather than processed hot with the addition of water. The intense sugar and flavor come through in full strength.

Grapes contain so much juice, though, that it's possible to nearly double the yield by processing the leftover skins and pulp with water, and extracting even more delicious juice. This second-run juice may be darker colored and tangy rather than ultrasweet, and it, too, can be used immediately or processed in a variety of ways.

Makes approximately 4 quarts

PREP TIME: 2–4 hours, plus canning

INGREDIENTS

20–25 pounds of ripe grapes (about 5 gallons of fruit)

Ascorbic acid, ¼ teaspoon per quart of juice (for canning)

Sugar, 2–4 tablespoons per quart of juice (optional, for canning)

1. Wash the fruit, and remove any stems or bad fruit.

2. Working in small batches, grind the fruit with a grinder attachment and empty the fruit into the basket of the fruit press. Assemble the pressing mechanism and press according to manufacturer's instructions. Collect the juice.

This juice can be used immediately or preserved by canning, freezing, or fermenting.

OPTIONAL SECOND RUN:

1. Retain the solids from the pressing and, working in small batches, process in the food processor.

2. Hang the solids in a juice bag made of several layers of cheesecloth. Let additional juice drip into a bowl overnight. Do not squeeze the bag.

3. Let the second-run juice settle overnight in the refrigerator, and drink or process to preserve.

4. The spent grape skins themselves contain yeast nutrients that help in winemaking; keep some in the refrigerator for later use. (They keep indefinitely, but if mold appears, throw them out.)

Cook's Tip:

Add a pint of grape cider, rather than pineapple juice, to any party punch.

CANNING NOTES

- Measure the juice by carefully ladling it off the sediments. Pour the measured juice into a nonreactive stockpot.

- Simmer juice at 190°F for 5 minutes. Remove from heat.

- Add sugar, if using (2–4 tablespoons per quart), and stir to dissolve.

- Add ascorbic acid to sterilized jars (¼ teaspoon per quart).

- Fill the jars with liquid, leaving ¼ inch of headspace. Apply sterilized lids and bands, being careful not to overtighten. Process both pint and quart jars in boiling-water bath for 15 minutes, adjusting for altitude (page 63).

crab
apple
juice

TANGY AND JUST A BIT TART, this is apple juice with attitude. We love the complex play of flavors: not too sweet, not too sour, just right. Although Crab Apple Juice certainly has apple overtones, the flavor is all its own. The color is an incomparably warm pink-orange that reflects the crab apples' rosy skin tones.

Not all crab apples are equal, and certainly not all of them deserve the fruit's reputation as too sour to eat. Several varieties have delectable flavor and lots of juice for processing: Callaway Crab, Kerr, and Dolgo. To test if your crab apples are tasty, pick a few, cut them in half to see if they are ripe (see page 82), cook the ripe ones for 10 minutes in enough water to cover, and then taste. If they are too tart, add a bit of sugar. If tasty, then use them in this recipe. If the crab apples taste bitter, do not use them.

Drink the juice at full strength, or add a soda mixer or vodka to create your own Crabby-tini. Crab Apple Juice can also be a component in any mixed fruit drink: try it with pear, apple, or grape juice.

Makes approximately 7 quarts

PREP TIME: About 2 hours, plus canning

INGREDIENTS

8–12 pounds of fresh crab apples (about 1 gallon), cut in half, bad parts cut out or discarded

Filtered water

Ascorbic acid, ¼ teaspoon per quart of juice (for canning)

Sugar, 2–4 tablespoons per quart of juice (optional, for canning)

1. Put the crab apples into a large nonreactive stockpot, and then add filtered water to cover the fruit by about a ½ inch. Bring the contents to a boil.

2. Reduce the heat and simmer for 10 minutes, stirring and mashing the fruit as it cooks. Stir occasionally to avoid sticking, and skim off any foam.

3. Line a large colander with two layers of cheesecloth that have been dampened with filtered water. Set the colander over a large bowl, making sure that the colander sits well above the bottom of the bowl so the juice can flow freely.

4. Slowly pour the hot crab apple liquid into the cheesecloth-lined colander.

5. Leave the juice to strain for 1 hour or more. Do not squeeze or force the crab apples through the cheesecloth, or the juice will become cloudy.

This juice can be used immediately or preserved by canning.

TO TEST FOR RIPENESS, cut a crab apple in half and look at the seed color. If the seeds are light colored, the fruit is not ripe. When the fruit is ready to harvest, the seeds turn brown.

CANNING NOTES

- Measure the juice by carefully ladling it off the sediments. Pour the measured juice into a nonreactive stockpot.

- Simmer juice at 190°F for 5 minutes. Remove from heat.

- Add sugar, if using (2–4 tablespoons per quart), and stir to dissolve.

- Add ascorbic acid to sterilized jars (¼ teaspoon per quart).

- Fill the jars with liquid, leaving ¼ inch of headspace. Apply sterilized lids and bands, being careful not to overtighten. Process both pint and quart jars in boiling-water bath for 15 minutes, adjusting for altitude (page 63).

apple juice

INGREDIENTS

15–20 pounds of fresh apples, quartered, bad parts cut out

Filtered water

Ascorbic acid, ¼ teaspoon per quart of juice (for canning)

Sugar, 2–4 tablespoons per quart of juice (optional, for canning)

APPLE JUICE IS DIFFERENT from our Apple Family Cider (page 85). The juice comes from apples that are cooked with filtered water and then strained, whereas apple cider is pressed raw and without any water added. Apples can be a bountiful harvest, so don't overload your pot and bowls and don't make your juice bag too heavy.

The flavor will vary with the kinds of apples used, and whether you use just one kind of apple or a mixture. A mix of tart apple varieties makes the best juice; sweet varieties or using a single variety can produce juice that seems bland or flat in comparison but is still worthwhile.

This pleasant juice carries the aroma of an open meadow, and its smooth, mild flavor makes it a perfect everyday drink for children.

Makes approximately 4 quarts

PREP TIME: About 2 hours, plus canning

1. Put the apples into a large nonreactive stockpot, and then add filtered water to cover the fruit by about ½ inch. Bring the contents to a boil.

2. Reduce the heat and simmer for 10 minutes, stirring and mashing the apples as they cook. Stir occasionally to avoid sticking, and skim off any foam.

3. Line a large colander with two layers of cheesecloth that have been dampened with filtered water. Set the colander over a large bowl, making sure that the colander sits well above the bottom of the bowl and the juice can flow freely.

4. Slowly pour the hot apple liquid into the cheesecloth-lined colander.

5. Leave the juice to strain for 1–2 hours. Do not squeeze or force the apples through the cheesecloth, or the juice will become cloudy.

This juice can be used immediately or preserved by canning.

Cook's Tip

This juice is very mild and may taste bland when first made without the addition of more sugar, so heat the juice with mulling spices for a winter treat. For the adults, add rum and a touch of butter. With or without added sugar, the flavor of canned apple juice seems to deepen and improve after a few months.

CANNING NOTES

- Measure the juice by carefully ladling it off the sediments. Pour the measured juice into a nonreactive stockpot.

- Simmer juice at 190°F for 5 minutes. Remove from heat.

- Add sugar, if using (2–4 tablespoons per quart), and stir to dissolve.

- Add ascorbic acid to sterilized jars (¼ teaspoon per quart).

- Fill the jars with liquid, leaving ¼ inch of headspace. Apply sterilized lids and bands, being careful not to overtighten. Process both pint and quart jars in boiling-water bath for 15 minutes, adjusting for altitude (page 63).

cider

juice

apple family cider

CIDER IS THE PURE PRESSED JUICE of fresh fruit, not juice extracted by cooking. The difference is immense in flavor, in feel, and in uses. Apples or crab apples make wonderful cider, especially when you mix different varieties.

Don't rush to start pressing fruit, however, until you know the full story (see Using a Fruit Press, page 56). Pressing fruit requires more time, money, and muscle than do other methods of extracting juice. First, you must have a lot of fruit at once: at least 5 gallons by volume to run a press effectively. Next, you need a fruit press plus a grinder to crush the fruit before pressing. And you need plenty of time and strength to operate and clean up the pressing equipment.

With those provisos, here's a recipe that produces excellent cider for drinking, canning, freezing, or fermenting.

Makes approximately 2–6 quarts

PREP TIME: 4–6 hours, plus canning

INGREDIENTS

25–40 pounds of mixed fall apple varieties, including tart apples and crab apples

Ascorbic acid, ¼ teaspoon per quart of juice (for canning)

1. Wash the fruit, and remove any leaves and damaged or rotten fruit.

2. Cut the fruit into halves or quarters. Working in small batches, grind the fruit with a grinder attachment or food processor, and empty the fruit into the basket of the fruit press.

3. Assemble the pressing mechanism according to the manufacturer's instructions. Collect the juice.

This juice can be used immediately or preserved by canning, freezing, or fermenting.

Cook's Tip

Fresh-pressed Apple Family Cider is naturally sweet and in our opinion needs no additional sugar. However, for canning — and canning only — the addition of a little ascorbic acid will go a long way to preserve the fabulous color and flavor of the product.

CANNING NOTES

- Measure the juice by carefully ladling it off the sediments. Pour the measured juice into a nonreactive stockpot.

- Simmer juice at 190°F for 5 minutes. Remove from heat.

- Add ascorbic acid to sterilized jars (¼ teaspoon per quart).

- Fill the jars with liquid, leaving ¼ inch of headspace. Apply sterilized lids and bands, being careful not to overtighten. Process both pint and quart jars in boiling-water bath for 15 minutes, adjusting for altitude (page 63).

peerless pear cider

INGREDIENTS

30–40 pounds of pears, cut in half and any bad or damaged spots removed

Ascorbic acid, ¼ teaspoon per quart of juice (for canning)

Sugar, 2–4 tablespoons per quart of juice (optional, for canning)

PEARS HAVE A BIG SECRET: They are full, full, full of juice! They can produce huge quantities of delicious pure cider (more than apples, in fact) that tastes almost tropical, with banana undertones and a nutty sweetness. The color is surprising, too; the ripe flesh of pears is nearly white but oxidizes to practically brick red as soon as it is ground and pressed.

Drink some of your pear cider right away, can some to save in the pantry, and turn some into perry, or fermented pear product (see chapter 5). And be sure to hang on to the pressed pear mash to make Happy Time Pear Juice, page 88. This recipe calls for a fruit grinder rather than a food processor, since pears can overwhelm the processor motor.

By the way, quinces also make good cider, either alone or mixed with pears.

Makes approximately 8 quarts

PREP TIME: 4–6 hours, plus canning

1. Working in small batches, grind the fruit in a grinder attachment and collect the mash in a large container. (Optional: let this mash sit overnight, covered and at room temperature, before pressing, to intensify the flavor.)

2. Empty the fruit into the basket of the fruit press.

3. Assemble the pressing mechanism and press according to manufacturer's instructions. Collect the juice.

4. Strain and store overnight in the refrigerator so that solids will settle.

This juice can be used immediately or preserved by canning.

CANNING NOTES

- Measure the juice by carefully ladling it off the sediments. Pour the measured juice into a nonreactive stockpot.

- Simmer juice at 190°F for 5 minutes. Remove from heat.

- Add sugar, if using (2–4 tablespoons per quart), and stir to dissolve.

- Add ascorbic acid to sterilized jars (¼ teaspoon per quart).

- Fill the jars with liquid, leaving ¼ inch of headspace. Apply sterilized lids and bands, being careful not to overtighten. Process both pint and quart jars in boiling-water bath for 15 minutes, adjusting for altitude (page 63).

Cook's Tip

A pear that's golden and feels soft to the touch is actually overripe, since pears ripen from the inside. And while pears can cling to the branches until a hard frost, once they hit the ground they perish rapidly and get devoured by bees and ants. It may take a couple of expeditions to get the amount of fruit needed for this recipe, but it's all right to mix green pears with those already ripening.

happy time pear juice

Makes approximately 10 quarts

PREP TIME: About 2 hours, plus overnight for juice to settle, plus canning

INGREDIENTS

Leftover mash from pressing 30–40 pounds pears, or 20–25 pounds chopped ripe pears

Filtered water

Ascorbic acid, ¼ teaspoon per quart of juice (for canning)

Sugar, 2–4 tablespoons per quart of juice (optional, for canning)

PEAR JUICE IS SIMILAR to apple juice, and known for its mild, sweet flavor. Happy Time Pear Juice comes from reusing the chopped pears from Peerless Pear Cider, page 86; we think of it as happy because it means a higher overall yield from the fruit. But you don't need to go to all the trouble of pressing pears to get pear juice. Just chop fresh pears into pieces and then use the heat extraction method.

1. **Put the crushed** pears into a large nonreactive stockpot, and then add filtered water to cover the fruit by about a ½ inch. Bring the contents to a boil.

2. **Reduce the heat** and simmer for 10 minutes, stirring and mashing the pears as they cook. Stir occasionally to avoid sticking, and skim off any foam.

3. **Line a large** colander with two layers of cheesecloth that have been dampened with filtered water. Set the colander over a large bowl, making sure that the colander sits well above the bottom of the bowl and the juice can flow freely.

4. **Slowly pour the** hot pear liquid into the cheesecloth-lined colander.

5. **Leave the juice** to strain overnight or at least 4 to 6 hours. Do not squeeze or force the pears through the cheesecloth, or the juice will contain too much pulp.

This juice can be used immediately or preserved by canning.

Cook's Tip

Pears are especially heavy, so you may have to break your produce into smaller batches. Otherwise cooking and straining can take forever.

CANNING NOTES

- Measure the juice by carefully ladling it off the sediments. Pour the measured juice into a nonreactive stockpot.

- Simmer juice at 190°F for 5 minutes. Remove from heat.

- Add sugar, if using (2–4 tablespoons per quart), and stir to dissolve.

- Add ascorbic acid to sterilized jars (¼ teaspoon per quart).

- Fill the jars with liquid, leaving ¼ inch of headspace. Apply sterilized lids and bands, being careful not to overtighten. Process both pint and quart jars in boiling-water bath for 15 minutes, adjusting for altitude (page 63).

prickly pear cactus juice

PRICKLY PEAR CACTUS GROWS as a wildflower across much of North America, and the pears — the lustrous magenta fruits called apples or tunas — too often go to waste. It's no wonder, really, since the fierce spines covering the cactus are a real deterrent. But carefully processed, the juice is delicious and holds no threat of stray fibers.

Pay attention to these harvesting guidelines: Dress in heavy-duty clothing and gloves, and go armed with long-handled tongs; the pears are easy to harvest in midautumn. You may find loads of prickly pears on patches of untended urban wilderness or along country roads, and it takes no time at all to gather a big basket full. The fruit yields a great deal of juice for its weight.

The juice of prickly pears differs from other juices because it runs in viscous threads instead of a stream of drops; the canning process removes that thickness. Be sure to use lots and lots of cheesecloth layers to strain out any stray plant spines from the juice.

Prickly pear juice has a light, clean, refreshing fruit flavor and is quite high in vitamin C, so we omit ascorbic acid for processing. Even without ascorbic acid added, this amazing juice held its color for a year. A little bit of sugar, however, brings out the full potential of this juice.

IMPORTANT: Under no circumstances use a fruit press for this recipe, only boiling water extraction, because tiny spines could lodge in parts of the press.

Makes approximately 6–8 quarts

PREP TIME: 2–3 hours, plus overnight for juice to settle, plus canning

INGREDIENTS

12–15 pounds ripe prickly pears

Filtered water

Sugar, 2–4 tablespoons per quart of juice (optional, for canning)

1. Rinse the pears in a colander and place them one by one, using tongs, into a large saucepan. Be careful not to touch the uncooked pears, as they have small spines.

2. Cover the pears with filtered water and bring to a boil.

3. Reduce heat and simmer for 10 minutes, stirring and mashing the pears as they cook, or use an immersion blender to grind the prickly pears and break apart the skins and release the juice.

Do not taste the juice until after it is strained, as it still contains tiny cactus spines!

4. Strain the juice through four layers of dampened cheesecloth over a large bowl. Strain again through four layers of additional (dampened) cheesecloth. Do not squeeze the pulp. Discard both sets of the cheesecloth.

5. Refrigerate overnight and ladle the juice off any remaining solids.

This juice can be used immediately or preserved by canning.

Cook's Tip

Prickly Pear Cactus Juice forms the basis of Prickly Pear Cactus Wine (page 146) and Prickly Pear Cactus Syrup (page 194). Add some to lemonade for a flavor and color boost.

CANNING NOTES

- Measure the juice by carefully ladling it off the sediments. Pour the measured juice into a nonreactive stockpot.

- Simmer juice at 190°F for 5 minutes. Remove from heat.

- Add sugar, if using (2–4 tablespoons per quart), and stir to dissolve.

- Fill the jars with liquid, leaving ¼ inch of headspace. Apply sterilized lids and bands, being careful not to overtighten. Process both pint and quart jars in boiling-water bath for 15 minutes, adjusting for altitude (page 63).

tomato juice

INGREDIENTS

20 pounds tomatoes (about 35 medium sized), quartered

Filtered water, enough to cover tomatoes

Lemon juice, 2 tablespoons per quart of tomato juice (for canning)

Salt, ¼ teaspoon per quart of tomato juice (for canning)

HOMEMADE TOMATO JUICE actually tastes like fresh tomatoes, not like the inside of a can. The consistency is quite a bit different from the thick supermarket variety. As the solids may settle, just shake the jar before pouring the juice.

Tomatoes have plenty of vitamin C, though the heat of processing destroys some of it. Still, during the winter the tasty juice acts as a tonic. If your garden produces tons and tons of tomatoes, here is one way to use them.

Makes approximately 2 quarts

PREP TIME: About 2 hours, plus overnight for juice to settle, plus canning

1. Put the tomatoes into a large nonre-active stockpot, and then add filtered water to cover the fruit by about ½ inch. Bring the contents to a boil.

2. Reduce the heat and simmer for 10 minutes, stir occasionally to avoid sticking, and skim off any foam.

3. Working in batches, purée the tomatoes in a food processor or blender or with an immersion blender until smooth.

4. Line a large colander with two layers of cheesecloth that have been dampened with filtered water. Set the colander over a large bowl, making sure that the colander sits well above the bottom of the bowl and the juice can flow freely.

5. Slowly pour the hot tomato liquid into the cheesecloth-lined colander.

6. Leave the juice to strain for at least 1 hour. Do not squeeze or force the tomatoes through the cheesecloth, or the juice will become too pulpy.

This juice can be used immediately or preserved by canning.

Cook's Tip

For canning, don't omit the salt unless you're on a low sodium diet, because it gives the flavor a big boost. If you're drinking this juice fresh, garnish with a dash of any gourmet salt.

CANNING NOTES

- Pour the measured juice into a nonreactive stockpot.

- Simmer at 190°F for 5 minutes. Remove from the heat.

- Meanwhile, add 2 tablespoons of lemon juice and ¼ teaspoon of salt to each sterilized quart jar (or 1 tablespoon of lemon juice and ⅛ teaspoon of salt to each pint jar). Then fill the jars with hot tomato juice, leaving ¼ inch of headspace. Apply sterilized lids and bands, being careful not to overtighten.

- Process both pint and quart jars in boiling-water bath for 15 minutes, adjusting for altitude (page 63).

sensational-7 vegetable drink

INGREDIENTS

FOR THE TOMATO JUICE

20 pounds tomatoes (about 35 medium sized), quartered

Filtered water, enough to cover tomatoes

FOR THE VEGETABLE JUICE

4–5 pounds tomatoes (about 10–14 medium sized), quartered

2 large carrots, peeled, coarsely chopped (about 1 cup)

1 large golden beet, peeled, coarsely chopped

1 large celeriac root (about ⅔ pound), peeled and chopped, or 6 ribs of celery, chopped

1 medium-to-large fennel bulb, trimmed and coarsely chopped

2 large garlic cloves, chopped

¼ cup fresh parsley leaves, chopped

2 bay leaves, fresh or dried

2 tablespoons coarse sea salt (or kosher salt)

6 tablespoons fresh lemon juice (¼ cup plus 2 tablespoons)

THIS RECIPE MAY LOOK LIKE a lot of work. After all, the first step is to make tomato juice. But the final result is so worth the extra time and effort that you may never want to taste store-bought vegetable-juice cocktail again. Sensational-7 Vegetable Drink combines all the spectacular flavors of midsummer in a magical concoction. If you preserve enough, it will keep you energized through the rest of the year.

Tomato juice by itself is rarely a crowd-pleaser because the taste is bland and flat without an awful lot of salt, sugar, or other flavor-stretching additives. Even picky vegetable eaters will enjoy this fresh vegetable drink, which packs a lot of ingredients — all of which you can grow yourself — into a simple treat that needs no accompaniment.

We offer a rather large-batch recipe here. But the truth is that when tomatoes are at their peak (and that can last for months) the quantities are unbelievable. There's no reason not to push a little and fix up enough to last a while.

Makes approximately 3 quarts

PREP TIME: About 2 hours, plus overnight for flavor development, plus canning

MAKE THE TOMATO JUICE

1. Put the tomatoes into a large non-reactive stockpot, and then add filtered water to cover by about ½ inch. Bring the contents to a boil.

2. Reduce the heat and simmer for 10 minutes, stir occasionally to avoid sticking, and skim off any foam.

3. Working in batches, purée tomatoes in a blender or with an immersion blender until smooth.

4. Line a large colander with two layers of cheesecloth that have been dampened with filtered water. Set the colander over a large bowl, making sure that the colander sits well above the bottom of the bowl and the juice can flow freely.

5. Slowly pour the hot tomato liquid into the cheesecloth-lined colander.

6. Leave the juice to strain for at least 1 hour. Do not squeeze or force the tomatoes through the cheesecloth, or the juice will become cloudy.

7. Refrigerate overnight, then combine with the vegetable juice to create the Sensational 7 Vegetable Drink.

MAKE THE VEGETABLE JUICE
(SAME DAY AS TOMATO JUICE)

1. Place all ingredients into a large nonreactive stockpot, and then add filtered water to barely cover (about 8 cups). Bring the contents to a boil.

2. Reduce the heat and simmer for about 40 minutes, or until all vegetables are soft. Stir occasionally to avoid sticking, and skim off any foam.

3. Discard bay leaves; add 2 tablespoons coarse salt and the lemon juice to the pot and let contents cool slightly.

4. Working in batches, purée the vegetable mixture in a blender until smooth. Refrigerate overnight to let the flavor develop.

COMBINE THE JUICES (DAY 2)
After both juices have been refrigerated, combine the vegetable mixture with the strained tomato juice.

This vegetable juice cocktail can be used immediately or preserved by canning.

CANNING NOTES

- Pour the measured juice into a nonreactive stockpot.

- Simmer the juice at 190°F for 5 minutes. Remove from heat.

- Meanwhile, add 2 tablespoons of lemon juice and ¼ teaspoon of salt to each sterilized quart jar (or 1 tablespoon of lemon juice and ⅛ teaspoon of salt to each pint jar). Then fill the jars with hot tomato juice, leaving ¼ inch of headspace. Apply sterilized lids and bands, being careful not to overtighten.

- Process both pint and quart jars in boiling-water bath for 15 minutes, adjusting for altitude (page 63).

Cook's Tip

Put up a few jars of the vegetable juice portion of this recipe and enjoy it as a soup base all winter.

deneice's super-heated bloody mary mixer

HERE'S A CAPITAL RECIPE, good with or without the addition of vodka or other spirits. There's no need to add extra spices, as there's a lot of heat already. Here are all the ingredients for a classic Bloody Mary mixer with lots of ground-up vegetables for a good bite.

The heat in this recipe comes from fresh horseradish (a garden staple if you have the room) and from garlic, cayenne pepper, and plenty of peppercorns. This recipe may be too hot for some people, although it does mellow with age. Reduce the spices by half to make a milder but just as tasty version of this recipe.

To make a good Bloody Mary, combine Bloody Mary mixer with gin or vodka at a ratio of 2 parts mixer to 1 part alcohol, or to taste. Serve over ice in a glass rimmed with celery salt or red pepper salt. Add freshly squeezed lime and pickled vegetables such as green beans, okra, pearl onions, or olives. Don't forget a fresh celery stalk to make the perfect cocktail.

Makes approximately 2 quarts

PREP TIME: About 2 hours, plus overnight for flavor development, plus canning

INGREDIENTS

- 4 pounds tomatoes (about 10 medium), quartered
- 2 large carrots, peeled and chopped
- 1 large golden beet, peeled and chopped
- 1 large celeriac root (about $2/3$ pound), peeled and chopped, or 6 ribs of celery, chopped
- 1 medium-to-large fennel bulb, trimmed and chopped
- 2 large garlic cloves, chopped
- ¼ cup fresh parsley leaves, chopped
- 2 bay leaves, rinsed
- 1 whole fresh cayenne pepper
  Filtered water
- 3 tablespoons coarse sea salt (or kosher salt)
- 6 tablespoons fresh lemon juice (¼ cup plus 2 tablespoons)
- 1 teaspoon celery seed
- ½ teaspoon mustard seed, coarsely ground
- ½ cup fresh horseradish, peeled, grated
- 2 tablespoons whole black peppercorns, coarsely ground
- ¾ cup Worcestershire sauce
- ½ cup hot pepper sauce, such as Tabasco, Crystal, or Texas Pete
- 1 tablespoon hot chili sauce, such as Sriracha
- ½ cup dark beer, such as stout or porter (optional)
  Lemon juice (for canning, 2 tablespoons per quart of juice)
  Salt (for canning, ¼ teaspoon per quart of juice)

1. **Place the tomatoes,** carrots, beet, celeriac root or celery, fennel, garlic, parsley, bay leaves, and cayenne pepper into a large nonreactive stockpot, and then add filtered water to barely cover (about 8 cups). Bring the contents to a boil.

2. **Reduce heat and** simmer for about 40 minutes, or until all vegetables are soft. Stir occasionally to avoid sticking, and skim off any foam.

3. **Discard bay leaves** and whole cayenne pepper; add 2 tablespoons of the coarse sea salt (or kosher salt); then add the lemon juice to the pot and let it cool slightly.

4. **Working in batches,** purée vegetable mixture in blender or with an immersion blender until smooth. Set aside.

5. **Grind celery and** mustard seeds with the remaining 1 tablespoon of coarse sea salt (or kosher salt) using a mortar and pestle or a spice grinder.

6. **Add the celery-seed-and-mustard** salt, the horseradish, the black pepper, the Worcestershire sauce, the hot pepper sauce, the hot chili sauce, and the beer (if desired) to the vegetable purée.

7. **Cover and chill** overnight for flavors to blend.

This juice can be used fresh or preserved by canning.

Cook's Tip

If you have fresh raw oysters on hand, drop one into a Bloody Mary to absorb the marvelous flavors; then enjoy the oyster once the drink is finished. Alternatively, garnish the glass with a boiled shrimp in the shell.

CANNING NOTES

- Pour the measured juice into a nonreactive stockpot.

- Simmer juice at 190°F for 5 minutes. Remove from heat.

- Meanwhile, add 2 tablespoons of lemon juice and ¼ teaspoon of salt to each sterilized quart jar (or 1 tablespoon of lemon juice and ⅛ teaspoon of salt to each pint jar). Then fill the jars with hot tomato juice, leaving ¼-inch headspace. Apply sterilized lids and bands, being careful not to overtighten

- Process both pint and quart jars in boiling-water bath for 15 minutes, adjusting for altitude (page 63).

5 creating wines, meads & specialty drinks

Wine, usually made from grapes, enlivens a panoply of social occasions and holds an important place at the dinner table and in some rituals. Commercial brands fill aisle after aisle of supermarkets, liquor stores, and gourmet shops. Even with all that variety, however, grape wines can seem predictable, even a little ho-hum.

Now it's time to bust out of the ordinary and explore the amazing world of homegrown garden wines. With its origins lost in the furthest reaches of time, winemaking has always tapped into local plant life. People have made wine from bountiful harvests of dates, rice, palm, bananas, yucca, potatoes, plums, pomegranates, and other staple crops. Gardeners and cooks everywhere can use what they grow to make the leap into fermented beverage production, turning their harvest into fresh new wines that will age beautifully in the pantry.

Let's get acquainted with various kinds of wines and other fermented beverages that were more common in centuries past, when people made wines out of anything and everything. Among the nongrape wines explored here are meads fermented with honey and flavorings, and hard ciders from fermented cold-pressed juices that are allowed to develop without appreciable added yeast or sugar. And while we don't discuss distilling at any length because home distillation is not legal in the United States, we do include one Old World recipe based on homegrown lemons (plus some store-bought spirits). Cheers!

OUR WINE MANIFESTO

WE DON'T LIKE TO BE RULED BY THE CLOCK OR THE CALENDAR. We prefer to adjust our personal schedules only to the growing season. Homegrown winemaking and other fermentation activities can take place virtually all year and in small, manageable quantities from ripening crops of flowers, herbs, fruits and berries, vegetables, leaves, and grains. Homegrown wines, ciders, and other fermented beverages exhibit seasonality; that is, they can be made in spring, summer, fall, or winter, depending on each ingredient's peak season for flavor, sugars, and so on. Some old-time winemakers used to put up their rose hip wine in fall and their carrot wine in the middle of winter, when the crops were sweetest.

WE USE SIMPLE, INEXPENSIVE EQUIPMENT AND SUPPLIES. There's no reason to spend much money getting started. Bottles can be recycled, and much of the other basic equipment may already be at hand. Fermentation requires little energy, because once the equipment is sanitized there is no more boiling to do. Wine "cooks" itself. All you may have to buy are yeast and sugar (or honey), some citrus fruit, and filtered water. And because any garden, no matter how small, will have something interesting to ferment, our method of fermented beverage production truly is for anyone, anywhere. If you grow lots of grapes, fine, make grape wine. But if you don't, there are plenty of other recipe choices.

THESE RECIPES CALL FOR JUICES YOU HAVE ALREADY MADE AND CANNED. What could be easier than popping open a jar of fruit juice that's already sitting in the cupboard, adding sugar and yeast, and putting the mixture in a dark closet for a few months to do its thing? It's so darn simple, and can take as little as half an hour to assemble. By using your canned juices for wine and mead, *you* become the scheduling boss.

a garden full of wine

HAVING ENJOYED MAKING garden wines ourselves, we think it's a magical experience that becomes more fulfilling with each passing year as we gain experience and confidence. Once you learn the principles of fermentation and learn about the basic equipment and skills, you can let your imagination take over.

There is no one exact right way to make fermented beverages. Much of the information handed down from generation to generation is downright contradictory. There's some elementary science at work, true, but over time winemaking becomes an art, a manner of personal expression that encompasses a vast and complex range of variables. Those variables can range from the duration of rainfall during the growing season, to the time of day you pick produce, to the amount of fertilizer in your soil.

Winemaking and its related activities are much like baking bread, and no more difficult. And just as temperature is crucial in canning juices, with all parts of the process required to take place at uniformly high readings, temperature is also crucial in winemaking. In winemaking, though, nothing must get too hot or too cold. There's a sweet spot in the middle that fosters the development of alcohol, and winemaking's key ingredient — yeast — must be activated in a lukewarm medium, just as it must for making leavened bread. Successful winemaking, like successful canning, does require strict sanitation, and we'll get into the details later in this chapter.

The recipes included here are ones we devised and tested in our own kitchens. Keep in mind that they are just a starting point for all your future endeavors. We have standardized these recipes for one-gallon batches so that home brewers can cut-and-paste to create their own specialties. You can match your harvest with any of these recipes to create your own unique personal brew.

what about beer?

This book doesn't address beer making at all. There are two reasons for that. The main ingredients for beer, malted cereal grains and hop flowers, don't fall easily into either the homegrown or farmers' market categories. And making beer requires strict timing, while winemaking is a lot more relaxed and flexible. Beer has a relatively short shelf life, too, whereas garden wines can age for years.

But take heart, beer lovers. Our recipe for Concentrated Watermelon Syrup (page 186) turned out, the first time we tried making it, as an almost jam-like paste that tasted strongly of pumpkins. Watermelon is a gourd, too; you could use the concentrated syrup to flavor homemade pumpkin ale. For that matter, any of our other syrup recipes might be useful for home brews.

the hardest part is patience

IF YOU ARE READY TO TRY making wine, mead, or hard cider, you may feel terrifically impatient to get the beverages into the bottles and then back out again. Sorry, but it's important to start making garden wines and then keep on making more of them before you've tasted the previous batch. Resist the temptation to sample your young, just-bottled garden wines, for you are sure to be disappointed. They will probably taste like bathtub brew! After all, the ingredients are raw; they are mixed but not truly blended by the hands of time.

If you wait a year or even two before opening the first bottle, though, you are likely to be wowed by the delicate mingling of flavors. It's the same idea as with a stew: always better the second day because the ingredients have had time to settle in together, to make whoopee in the dark. In the case of garden wines, the process takes a bit longer. At the very least, wait six months before testing the wares. Flower and herb wines take the least amount of time to come together in the bottle; fruit and berry wines perhaps longest.

Have faith: most of your efforts will be quite good, and you will learn from any setbacks. Fortunately, most problems

in fermentation are apparent at the beginning of the process, not the end. The entire fermentation process has lots of waiting time built in, especially with wine and mead rather than the quicker hard ciders.

With hard cider, though, experts recommend picking a large quantity of apples when they are good and ripe, and then piling them on a tarpaulin outdoors for up to two weeks before even grinding the fruit and pressing it. It turns out that apple flavor and fermentation characteristics improve in that gradual "setting up" stage.

So the apples have been piled up for two weeks. Now it's time to grind and press. That takes the better part of a day. Then you sanitize a fermentation vessel and airlock, throw in a few homegrown raisins, and let the ingredients begin their alcoholic dance of life. Assume that fermentation takes at least a month longer, and by now winter's snow may be falling.

Berry wine is another example. Once you have harvested and washed all the berries, it takes a very short time to process them and start the fermentation process. But it might be two or three months before the wine stops bubbling, and during that period you might have racked the product off the dregs a couple of times. Only then, when fermentation has slowed to almost nothing, can you bottle the results.

Now the clock starts ticking for a year or two, until the date arrives to decant your masterpiece. See? Making wine is not difficult, but it requires patience.

start small

Those big carboys (glass fermentation vessels with small, sturdy necks) are not very expensive. And they're cool to look at. So you may be thinking, why not buy one and start big? For one thing, a multi-gallon carboy filled with liquid is pretty heavy to move. And washing a carboy thoroughly can be a time-consuming job that requires a lot of hot water and specialized bottle brushes.

We think it's much more sustainable, in terms of space and labor, to make one-gallon batches. You can experiment with different recipes more easily, and if there's a failure in the fermentation process, you won't lose as much product as you would with a three or five-gallon batch. Having said that, we must acknowledge that some of our closest friends are big-batch aficionados.

They are the kind of folks who, when they suddenly come into a bushel or two of peaches or five gallons of blackberries, figure, "What the heck, let's go for it," and drag the biggest carboy out of the closet. For these confident winemakers the payoff is producing dozens of bottles of finished wine at once, rather than the smaller yield of a one-gallon jug.

Either way, once you find a recipe that really works for you, it might be time to ramp up, invest in bigger and better equipment, and undertake large-batch production generally. If you take this route, then think through the entire process of months or years, and be sure you know where everything will be stored along the way.

VISIT A HOME BREW SUPPLY STORE

Online shopping is certainly convenient for winemaking equipment and supplies, but consider the benefits of buying everything at a local home brew supply store, even if the cost is a few dollars more. The staff will be able to answer questions about the process and will likely welcome the chance to help beginners. That's priceless.

how fermentation works

THE BASIC EQUATION for making wine, mead, or cider is:

> Yeast + Sugar (or Honey) =
> Carbon Dioxide + Alcohol

This means that when properly activated, the yeast, which consists of living single-cell organisms, will consume the sugar in a juice mixture while creating a gas and an intoxicating compound — carbon dioxide (CO_2) and alcohol.

To release the CO_2 without introducing wild yeasts and bacteria from the air, you must stopper the fermentation vessel with a simple device called an airlock (or you can fake it with a small plastic bag and a not-too-tight rubber band). In essence, an airlock is a one-way vent. Thanks to a little bit of sanitized water held level in a plastic chamber above the fermentation vessel, the airlock lets carbon dioxide escape without any additional oxygen being able to reach the contents of the vessel.

After the most vigorous early fermentation has taken place (usually in a few days to a week), further oxygen can interrupt the fermentation process and spoil the wine. Once the alcohol content of the juice reaches a particular level, which varies from a low of 6 percent with hard cider to about 14 percent with some wines and up to 18 percent with some meads, the yeast can no longer live and fermentation stops. That's when you bottle the finished product.

Keep in mind that when the fermentation stops, any leftover sugar in the liquid will produce a sweet wine or a not-so-sweet wine, depending on the type of yeast used and how much remains undigested.

the role of yeast

The air around us is naturally full of yeast cells. Each one has the capacity, when moistened, warmed, and brought into contact with food (sugar or honey), to multiply wildly. Some types of yeast help create delicious fermented drinks; others make the juice undrinkable. So in fermentation for homegrown wines, the idea is to give the beneficial yeasts a boost so that they can overwhelm the undesirable ones right off the bat and prevent spoilage.

We'll talk about those yeast starters in more detail shortly, but let's just say that in a pinch you can use a packet of bread yeast to start any homegrown wine and the results might taste just fine. We have made wine and mead with both bread yeast and wine yeast, and we found the taste is better with the wine yeast.

The simple formula of Yeast + Sugar (or honey) = Carbon dioxide + Alcohol never varies. What does vary

THIS JUG of peach mead is still fermenting, as indicated by the foaming action of the yeast. At the bottom, a layer of sediment comprised of dead yeast cells, called the lees, has formed.

considerably are the ways you can put together the wine and mead recipes to capitalize on your fresh produce at hand.

In the case of herb or flower wines, the flavor component in a gallon of herb essence, or tea, is strong, but there's no naturally occurring beneficial yeast or sugar. Once those are added, fermentation can begin and the result will be wine. In contrast, lots of fruits and berries and even tree sap, including such exotics as prickly pear cactus juice and birch water, have plenty of flavor and sugar already. They just need the dissolved yeast and a nutrient such as raisins or fresh grape skins to sustain the process.

Finally, because pure juice from pears, apples, and grapes already contains a full complement of sugar, flavor, and yeast, these juices can actually be fermented without adding anything. As we will show, however, that practice of wild fermentation is risky because without some help at the start, rogue yeasts or bacteria can overwhelm the good yeast, which is not a pleasant thing.

different kinds of fermented drinks

ONE WAY TO LOOK at the main characteristics of various fermented garden beverages is to go from lowest to highest alcohol content.

hard cider

Sometimes called folk or farm cider, hard cider is made from the pure unheated and undiluted juice of any fruit, berry, or vine. We emphasize "unheated" because once any juice is brought to temperatures much over lukewarm, the naturally occurring yeasts will die and proper fermentation cannot take place unaided. If you made juice from boiling up fruit and straining the liquid, you can't make hard cider without adding yeast; the naturally occurring yeast has been killed. If you pressed the fruit in a screw press and never heated it, the wild yeast will remain.

Traditionally, hard ciders have neither yeast nor sugar added; they were allowed to begin their fermentation using the existing yeasts. However, to give yourself the best chances for a successful hard cider, it's perfectly all right to activate some brewing yeast with warmed juice, and pitch it in the fermentation vessel to kick up the pace. ("Pitch" is the technical term for adding yeast to start a fermentation.)

And you can make pear cider, which is called perry. Pears seem to harbor a lot of extra yeasts and other microbes on the skin, compared to apples, so pear cider is apt to need a boost of brewing yeast to overcome the tendency to become overwhelmed by unfriendly yeast spores and spoil . . . no good for drinking.

Crab apples, in contrast, have astringent tannins that can keep unwanted growths at bay, and so produce a superior hard cider in a short time without added yeast. When no additional yeast is added, hard ciders range from about 6 percent to 7.5 percent alcohol. Not a blast, but a good time for sure.

garden wines

Any good herb or flower can be steeped to produce a flavorful tea, to which you add sugar and yeast to produce wine. Another easy technique is to stuff fresh leaves or flower petals directly into the fermentation vessel before adding the sugar, yeast, and water at proper temperatures. Then just strain out the leaves later.

All of these garden wines top out at about 14 percent alcohol, with countless variables determining the exact percentage. We confess that we don't really care what the exact level is. Measuring precise sugar levels and alcohol levels does not fit into our way of doing things. Winemaking purists may disagree, but we don't think they're having as much fun as we are!

mead

Mead is a fermented fruit, herb, or flower beverage in which honey, rather than cane sugar, is fed to the yeast. The alcohol content can vary substantially, and may depend on the type of yeast used or the proportion of honey to water; some kinds of mead produce up to 18 percent alcohol, others as low as 11 percent, and still others even less. An expert at a home brew supply store can be a good adviser on types of yeast. The higher the alcohol content, the less chance there is that the mead can spoil.

There are numerous cousins within the mead family: **metheglin** is mead flavored with spices, **melomel** is mead fermented from fruit or berries, and **pyment** is mead from grapes. And there are dozens more specialty meads from around the world. For instance, **Viking Blood** is mead made of cherry juice, while **rhodomel** is mead from rose hips. You get the idea. We're going to call it all mead, if you don't mind.

Mead actually predates wine by many accounts, since honey is nature's original sweetener. It is savored all over the world in its many marvelous forms. The flavor is always rich and complex, often brushed with soft remnants of honey. When properly made, mead will come out crystal clear and sometimes sparkling with effervescence.

managing the must

YOU KNOW THE DRILL with fruit, flowers, herbs, leaves, and other fresh ingredients: pick carefully, wash carefully, handle carefully. With winemaking, there's another kind of ingredient. When fermenting fruit, herbs, or just about anything else, the first step is creating a balanced *must*, which is the unfermented mixture of fruit juice and sugar or honey to which the yeast is added.

Certain components beyond sugar, yeast, and flavor need to be present in your must for a complete and satisfying fermentation to happen, while other kinds should be minimized. Here is what you need to know about properly managing your must.

sugar

For straightforward winemaking, we recommend pure cane sugar as the default setting. You are welcome to experiment with brown sugar, palm sugar, or another sugar you like. Just be aware that anything other than pure cane sugar may impart a stronger taste than you care for in an herb or flower wine. Plus, white sugar is easy to store in quantity, easy to measure, and easy to pour into a carboy or jug. It dissolves quickly and doesn't cost much.

Mead is made with honey rather than sugar. Use raw or unrefined honey, not the commercial brands sold in the grocery store, which have been pasteurized, a process that kills off most of the natural yeast and will affect the flavor of your mead. The closer to home you can find honey for sale, the more authentic your mead will taste, with more of the microscopic bits of pollen that reflect the local flowers. Purchase honey in volume; quarts or even gallons are more economical than smaller jars. In recipes, honey is often called for in pounds — one quart equals a pound.

yeast

Centuries of human interaction with yeast have removed a lot of the guesswork from fermentation processes. Home brew supply stores carry varieties of dried yeast that are especially effective with different kinds of crops, available in small, easy-to-store packets. There are yeasts for white wine, red wine, fruit wine, Champagne-style wine, and so on. Many of our recipes specify white wine or Champagne yeast, but if you treat any yeast carefully it should work fine. We don't think the small difference in results is worth worrying about.

One thing to note: brewer's yeast is different from bread yeast; we do not recommend using the latter. Some experts say that using bread yeast keeps the alcohol level fairly low for wine, about 10 percent at the most. Bread yeast may also keep a wine from becoming perfectly clear. In other words, results are unpredictable.

TYPES OF YEAST

For simplicity, our recipes mostly specify Pasteur Champagne yeast as a default setting that should work with most any beverage fermentation. You may like to branch out and match different types of packaged wine yeast with specific kinds of garden drinks: Dry Mead yeast for dry ciders and meads, Bordeaux yeast for prickly pear cactus and other dark fruit wines, Eau de Vie yeast for light flower or herb wines, and Sake #9 yeast for fruit-laden rice wine.

yeast nutrients

Yeast needs some nutritional support to achieve best results in fermentation. Think of the way gasoline ignites explosively with a spark. When the arson squad arrives at a suspicious fire they are looking for accelerants, or substances that speed up and spread combustion. That's the idea with yeast nutrients. They're the accelerant for the slow burn of fermentation.

Yeast nutrients, which include nitrogen, vitamin B^1, and phosphate, are needed in small amounts. The skins of red grapes are nature's best yeast accelerant, and so nearly all our recipes include raisins. **Warning:** Do not use commercially grown golden raisins, which contain sulfur dioxide as a color and freshness preservative. The sulfur dioxide imparts an unpleasant flavor and can ruin your wines, meads, and ciders.

If raisins or grape skins are not on hand, you can buy commercial yeast nutrient from your local brew supply store. Use 1 teaspoon per gallon of the nutrient for both wine and mead. One advantage commercial yeast nutrient has over raisins is that it will not affect the taste of the beverage. Both raisins and grape skins will add to the final flavor of your wine or mead.

Ironically, there will be a greater need for yeast nutrients in the crops you harvest from the wild or from sections of your garden that don't have much fertilizer added. The crops from well-manured sections of the garden will naturally contain more nitrogen than wild or unfertilized plants will.

tannins

Tannins are astringent compounds that occur on fruit skins, notably grape skins, and in fact on most plants before their fruits and leaves are fully developed. Think of tannins as a magic wand waving back and forth across the bottles: In fermenting beverages, tannins help blend flavors and help prolong shelf life of wines and keep them clear.

If you are making grape wine, there are tannins galore already. However, herb or flower wines, especially, may benefit from the addition of a cup of brewed tea to the mixture, white tea if you like (full disclosure: We have not tried this tea-added method). A number of our fermentation recipes suggest adding grape skins or raisins, partly to increase tannin levels. And a shout-out for our favorite fruit of all: crab apples. These crispy, juicy little apples have a lot of tannins and make a no-worry base for many fermented beverages.

SAVE THOSE SKINS!

In some cases we specifically mention grape skins rather than commercial raisins; that's because if you press your own grapes at home you will have lots of goopy grape skins left over. Pack some of them in wide-mouth pint jars and store them in the refrigerator for up to two weeks or in the freezer for up to a year so that you can pull out the yeasty, tannin-packed, nutrient-rich skins as you need them, to add to any fermentation vessel.

acidity

A degree of acidity is required in wine-making, both to help get fermentation started and to protect the developing wine from bacterial damage and from excess oxidation. Acidity helps balance the character of wine and other fermented beverages. We don't actually measure the acidity level of our home-made beverages (we won't tell if you don't), but strict winemakers often do so with a special kit.

Instead, most of our fermented recipes include lemons or oranges. If you don't have access to homegrown, use organic citrus fruits that are not coated with wax or oil so that the zesty peels are pristine, or scrub any coated fruit gently but thoroughly.

In the delicate balancing act of wine chemistry, sweet wines have higher acidity requirements than dry wines. Go figure. In nature, fruits with the highest natural acid levels include all berries, quince, currants, and rhubarb. Next come orchard fruits like apples, peaches, plums, and cherries. And lowest are pears, flowers, herbs, root crops, and (surprisingly) rose hips.

pectin

Pectin is the elusive gelatinous substance that gives fruits the ability to jell, to hold together in all their liquid glory. But pectin is cloudy and so is not desirable in wine or some other fermented beverages. Apples have a lot of pectin, which, along with oxidation, gives apple cider its characteristic dense appearance. We adore a pectin-rich cider, but when it comes to finer wines and meads, no thanks.

One complication in countering high pectin is that boiling fruit to make juice breaks down an enzyme that otherwise would consume pectin, which can result in a hazy appearance in the final product. In the end, a high pectin level in a beverage is more an aesthetic handicap than a real problem, but there are several specific pectin-busting techniques you can try. For starters, heating the fruit to lukewarm before grinding and pressing it can accelerate the digestion of pectin. Letting a juice extract sit overnight allows all sorts of junk to settle to the bottom of the container, and then you can ladle out the clear liquid.

If neither of those techniques does the trick, a local brew shop can supply you with perfectly safe enzyme additives to "fine," or clarify, your wine before bottling. Believe it or not, the clearing enzymes are sometimes made of things like shrimp skeletons, fish bladders, and such. In olden times people used egg-shells to clarify wine — we tried it and it worked! It took two weeks, but the wine cleared up nicely.

water

It is necessary to use a little bit of water even with full-juice wines like grape. As noted earlier, we recommend filtered water rather than straight tap water in all of our recipes. In herb or flower wines, and in many fruit wines, we suggest using filtered water to produce the essence for fermentation. You will also use filtered water, or better yet, a sanitizing solution, in the airlock so nothing naughty sneaks down into the fermentation vessel.

topping-up liquid

Excess oxygen is the enemy of fermenting beverages, although yeast requires some oxygen to get started. That is why fermentation vessels, whether large carboys or gallon jugs, have wide shoulders and narrow necks. The idea is that once fermentation begins, causing some liquid to bubble out of the vessel, you can top up the bubbling mixture with filtered water or juice to keep the air space as small as possible. Try to keep your fermenting beverages filled far up in the neck of the vessel.

That first, very active and sometimes messy, aerobic fermentation takes place while the newly activated yeast consumes the relatively small amount of oxygen in the headspace and dissolved in the liquid. This phase of fermentation is almost violent, within the confines of the bottle. It's not unusual for a cup or more of liquid to push right out of the airlock, so keep the jug in a baking pan to minimize mess. The anaerobic fermentation that follows, when the yeast is eating the sugar in the liquid, is sedate by comparison. It is during this

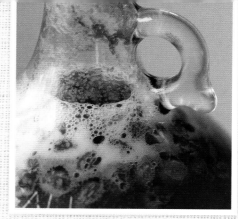

THE FIRST FERMENTATION can be quite messy. Here you can see the activity at the top of the carboy; the raisins give the yeast added sugar to munch.

phase that it's important to keep oxygen from entering the must.

If you can, reserve some of your fruit juices by refrigeration or canning to use as topping-up liquid during the early fermentation stage. Of course, if necessary you can top up with filtered water to minimize oxygen in the jug, but we like to keep the flavors strong. Unless you're a purist, you can use any kind of fruit juice for topping up, since it will contain all sorts of goodies like sugar and nutrients. Will anyone really notice if you add a pint of serviceberry juice or peach juice to a gallon or more of fermenting herb wine or mead?

In the case of herb or flower wines, your topping-up liquid could be a freshly brewed pint of tea to match. That way the flavor stays pure. In practice, herb or flower wines may not show as much active bubbling as fruit wines.

how to make wine

WITH ALL YOUR INGREDIENTS assembled and a recipe in hand, it's time to start fermenting. Our recipes call for a one-gallon glass jug, measuring cups, a large funnel, and an airlock with the proper size rubber stopper (sometimes called a bung). Later you will need a second jug or other holding vessel for racking. This process also requires a four-foot length of clear plastic tubing and a rigid plastic pipe called a racking cane, which has a special tip to keep the cane from sucking up the dregs.

KEEPING A POT of sanitizer on hand makes it easy to quickly sanitize small items and clean your hands before touching anything.

sanitizing the equipment

It is crucially important to clean *and* sanitize your equipment just before using it. You may be wondering, "What's the difference?"

Cleaning means to remove any dirt, dust, grime, oils, or any chunks of old yeast or fruit sugars from every piece of equipment. Wash with mild soap and hot water, using bottle brushes as necessary. Everything must be spotless!

Sanitizing, which destroys any remaining bacteria or other microbes, can be done by rinsing the carboy with lots of boiling water, or employing one of many easy-to-use chemical means. The simplest is a dilute solution of household bleach, 1 tablespoon per 5 gallons of warm water (for a large carboy) or

1 teaspoon per 1 gallon. Fill the vessel with the solution, swish it around, empty it, fill with plain warm water and rinse twice more to remove any residue of chlorine that could affect the wine's taste.

Another option is Star San, a solution used by home brewers. Use as directed and don't be put off by the fact that it appears bubbly. It is not meant to be rinsed off before you use the sanitized equipment.

There's also a magic pill called the Campden tablet, available inexpensively at home brew supply stores. The instructions will tell you how many tablets to crush and dissolve. Unlike chlorine bleach, Campden tablets leave no risk of aftertaste and requires less rinsing. A home brew supply store may have other kinds of sanitizing chemicals in tablet form, and there are some good no-rinse liquid sanitizers.

Any fermentation trouble you encounter is likely to be caused by lack of sanitation. It takes very little bacteria in the bottom of an imperfectly cleaned bottle to ruin a batch of wine. Every time you handle the contents or equipment of an ongoing fermentation there is danger of introducing bacteria, stray yeast, or other undesirable germs. Transferring contents back and forth between vessels, while necessary to remove sediments, creates risk.

So remember to sanitize all equipment you use *every* step of the way, including the bottles and bottling equipment you use once fermentation is complete. And *after* use, wash and air-dry the equipment, and store it in a cupboard; at the very least put a plastic bag over the mouth of any jugs or carboys to keep germs from entering. Some winemakers put a drop of bleach and a tablespoon or so of water into a vessel during storage.

proofing the yeast

Dried yeast should be stored in a refrigerator or other cool, dry place until it is needed. Your yeast may be stamped with a "use by" date; some vintners say to discard it if that date has expired, but it's worth a try first to see if the yeast still has life in it (see Troubleshooting Guide for Fermentation, page 128).

When you are ready to use it, yeast needs some kind of sugary, lukewarm liquid to unleash its fermentation power. Generally, to proof (or activate) the yeast, our recipes call for adding one ½-ounce packet of dry yeast (2 rounded teaspoons) to a cup of lukewarm fruit juice. You can also add the yeast to a cup of warm water plus one or two tablespoons of either sugar, jelly, or syrup.

No matter what, you should see the yeast begin to foam and bubble within a few minutes. If it just sits there like powder, something's wrong: The water may be too cold or too hot, or the yeast may have expired, or if unfiltered, the water itself may have high chlorine or other chemical levels. If it *does* start bubbling away, let the proofed yeast sit for at least 10 more minutes before adding it to a fermentation vessel containing the *must*. At this point, the must, too, should be no more than lukewarm.

CAREFUL WITH THAT HOT WATER

Heat cleaning is highly effective, but if the equipment is too hot when the yeast first touches it, the yeast may die. That's no good! Be sure to let all the pieces cool off to lukewarm before adding the yeast.

During the fermentation process, store your vessels in a quiet place without bright light. The temperature must remain between 60°F and 75°F; the ideal is about 65°F. Wine can take on unpleasant tastes if fermentation occurs at high temperatures, and at low temperatures the yeast action may slow to a crawl or stop. The same temperature range holds for storing finished bottled wines.

Many old wine recipes use a piece of toast as a starting medium for the activated yeast. In that method, you pour the proofed yeast onto a piece of toast, and then insert the toast into the fermentation vessel; this would work better with a large carboy than a gallon jug. Pour any remaining proofed yeast into the vessel, too. The toast, with its grains and sugars, can act as a yeast nutrient.

fermentation

After preparing your equipment, the next step is to put all the ingredients, including activated yeast (see Proofing the Yeast, 113), into a one-gallon glass jug and apply the airlock. Put the jug in a dark spot with the temperature between 65 and 75°F; don't jostle the jug but check on it within an hour or two. If all goes well, you'll see something amazing, something wonderful: foaming, churning movement, a sign of life. We admit to gazing with adoration at a jug of newly fermenting

juice, putting our ears to the glass to hear the tiny bubbles rising to the top, even getting up in the night to check on the new "baby."

The primary fermentation begins the process by admitting oxygen for the yeast to consume as it begins to multiply rapidly. This stage is sometimes called aerobic fermentation (meaning "with oxygen") for just that reason. Within a few days the fermentation can be absolutely wild (especially with potato wine), with yeasty foam and bits of fruit and juice gushing up through the airspace and into the airlock.

Also during this active phase of fermentation you will see gunk that precipitates from the liquid and forms a layer like undersea sand on the bottom of the jug. The whole thing can look like an awful mess . . . but just wait and see what happens.

Sometimes fermentation is so active that you may need to remove the airlock, clean it, and sanitize it again. If you don't, a rampant bacterial growth could spoil the wine. When you reassemble the airlock, be sure to wipe down the outside surfaces of the jug with a sanitizing solution, for example a drop of bleach with water on a clean cloth, or a water–Campden tablet solution. Every bit of fruit juice left outside a fermenting jug is an open house invitation for wild yeast and bacteria to party down at your expense.

AN ALTERNATIVE METHOD

It's important to note that our method for this early stage of fermentation is not the only way. Many antique recipes call for several days of fermentation in an open crock or jug, with only a layer of muslin or several layers of cheesecloth — no airlock yet — to keep out fruit flies and their attendant germs.

This method avoids some of the airlock mess but leaves the mixture subject to airborne contamination. You still have to transfer all the contents into a carboy at this messy stage, since an airlock will have to be applied eventually.

Brewing specialists are divided on which method to use, but to avoid contamination of the wine or mead with wild yeast, we prefer to go ahead and stopper the jug or carboy with the airlock as soon as all the ingredients are mixed and there are signs of active fermentation. Then clean up as needed.

1

2

3

4

1. To make the Mixed Berry Mead (recipe on page 154) shown here, start by activating the yeast. Heat one cup of any fruit juice to lukewarm (105°F) and sprinkle the yeast on top. Set it aside to do its thing; mixing is fine but not required. After a few minutes the yeast will begin to bubble and foam.

2. Wines can be started with any type of juice or cider, or a tea made from herbs. Here, frozen berries are covered with water and brought to a boil, then simmered to extract the juice.

3. First into the carboy is the sweetener – honey for mead or sugar for wine. The raisins go in at this point as well.

4. Add about half of the hot juice to the honey to dissolve it. Wine recipes often call for just a cup or two of hot juice in this step, because the sugar dissolves more easily.

5. Swirl the carboy vigorously to dissolve the honey. The action also adds oxygen to the liquid, which helps the first stage of fermentation.

6. Pour in the rest of the juice, leaving enough room (4 to 6 inches) at the top to add the yeast. Allow the carboy to cool to lukewarm.

continued

7. Once all the yeast has sifted to the bottom of the cup and is bubbling away, give it a quick stir and pour it into the carboy. Top off the carboy with any remaining juice, leaving just 2 or 3 inches of headspace.

8. Put a few tablespoons of filtered water or Star San in the airlock. Wipe off any spills with a clean cloth, then apply the stopper and airlock. Put the carboy in a cool dark space to ferment, checking in an hour or so that the airlock is bubbling.

9. After a few days, the juice may have changed color and the action of the yeast will have thrown up all kinds of debris. When a layer of spent yeast becomes visible on the bottom of the vessel, it's time to rack off to a clean one.

TAKE NOTES, LOTS OF NOTES!

It's essential to use some system to keep track of all the steps you take with your wines, meads, and other fermented beverages. All those jugs begin to look alike before long, so you need a way to record the starting date, racking dates, any topping-up liquid or nutrients added, and so on. Get in the habit of recording each step of the fermentation when it happens. Over time, such notes give you a feel for how long a batch of this or that will take, and what ingredients give the most enjoyable results.

One elegant method is to tie a stout notecard around the neck of the fermenting vessel, noting all relevant information in order. Another, less sexy way is to label each fermentation vessel with a number and then log information onto a master notebook.

Our favorite way is to use gaudy-colored stick-on notes slapped on each vessel as we work. If you make any deviations from a written recipe, record the changes on these notes. Quick and easy to transfer, these notes tell the tale.

Here are the notes from a typical batch of Easy Garden Grape Wine, describing the contents, additions, and activity of the wine:

A second example shows the notes from our first attempt at Prickly Pear Cactus Wine:

EASY GARDEN GRAPE WINE
- Start 9/24/12
- Contents: muscadine cider w/yeast
- First racked 9/28/12, added 1 quart muscadine grapes and cider together
- Top up with muscadine + cider added 1/4 c. grape skins
- Second rack 10/15/12
- Third rack 11/17/12
- Bottled 1/15/13

PRICKLY PEAR CACTUS WINE
- Start 10/15/12
- Contents: 2 quarts Prickly Pear Cactus Juice, grape skins, yeast
- First rack 10/21/12
- Second rack 11/17/12 added 1/2 cup serviceberry juice added filtered water to bring 3/4 gallon back to 1 gallon
- Final rack and bottle 2/1/13

On September 24, 2012, we pressed the juice and began primary fermentation. Four days later the fermentation was so vigorous that we racked the wine (9/28/12), adding more liquid and some grape skins. Three weeks later (10/15/12) and again a week after that (11/17/12), it needed racking again. After that, things really slowed down, and the jug sat undisturbed under a desk with no more notes. By late December 2012 that gallon jug of wine had cleared, but we let it sit for another month before we bottled it (1/15/13), just for convenience.

We started the wine in mid-October with juice we had just extracted from a gallon of prickly pears. We did not add sugar or citrus, only a few grape skins, since prickly pear juice is already sweet and high in vitamin C. Less than a week later it was time to rack the wine (10/21/12), and again three weeks later (11/17/12). At that time we added berry juice and enough filtered water to bring the volume up from 3/4 gallon to a whole gallon. Then fermentation slowed down and we waited until well into the New Year to rack a final time and to bottle the wine (2/1/13).

racking

IT MAY TAKE SEVERAL WEEKS to several months for your wine or mead to ferment entirely and reach the point where you can bottle it. During that time you will probably need to rack the wine; that is, siphon the fermenting liquid from the first jug or carboy into a second one, leaving the dregs behind. The idea is to remove the still-fermenting beverage from spent organic material so that the beverage can clear. The dregs, technically called the lees, appear as a light-colored layer of sludge on the bottom.

There are no hard and fast rules about when to start racking your wine, nor how often to rack it during fermentation. Many experts recommend doing the first racking within a week, and then it's up to you. In general you shouldn't rack wine more than about four times during active fermentation and before you bottle it.

There's a risk that the wine will "break down" under the stress of the process. However, racking wine allows it to clear by removing spent yeast from the mixture every so often. Leaving the spent yeast in the fermentation vessel can give wine a strong yeasty flavor.

keep it clean

Again, it's vitally important to clean and sanitize all the equipment — namely, a second vessel for continuing fermentation, a clean airlock, a racking cane, and a four-foot length of clear plastic tubing to fit the cane. Also, keep rags handy during racking, because something always spills.

Racking uses gravity to pull the clear liquid from the first vessel into the second one. In order for the liquid to begin flowing, the hose must be primed or filled with fluid. With the first vessel higher than the second, the primer liquid flows to the lower one, pulling the cleared wine or mead with it. You can use a siphon pump to begin this process (as shown on page 122) or, if you don't have a pump, you can prime the hose in a couple of other ways.

The simplest is to suck gently on the open end of the tubing and, when the fermenting liquid fills the tubing, stick the end of it on the bottom of the second vessel. We confess that this is our preferred method because it is quick and easy, but you do risk introducing bacteria to your wine. Another way is to fill the tubing with sterile water or juice to start the suction, then letting that liquid and the first bit of wine drain into the sink before pinching off the tube and moving it to the secondary fermenter.

sampling your progress

Do we sneak a taste of the wine when racking? Guilty as charged! It's too irresistible. If the wine already has a nice feel, we know the fermentation will take care of itself over time. If, however, the taste seems too tart or bitter, we know the wine may need either a lot of time in the bottle to blend or additional flavor or sugar.

We suggest buying a pipette to sample the progress of your wine or mead as it ferments. Home brew supply stores carry these straight glass tubes, which are about a foot long and a quarter inch in diameter. A plastic straw works just as well, however. Whichever you choose, sanitize it before testing your beverage for flavor.

- Remove the airlock and stopper from the jug and place them on a sanitized surface.

- Insert the pipette into the middle of the liquid; some will enter the tube.

- Place your thumb over the top of the pipe the to create a vacuum and hold the liquid in the pipette.

- Keeping your thumb on the opening, remove the pipette from the jug.

- Position the pipette over a small drinking glass and lift your thumb to release the liquid.

- Replace the stopper and airlock before you sip!

USING A HYDROMETER

As the yeast convert the sugar into alcohol, some winemakers like to track the process by methods other than guesswork or by look. Many winemaking books suggest using a hydrometer to measure the specific gravity (basically, the amount of sugar in the liquid) at the beginning of the fermentation and then periodically to gauge progress. To be honest, we've never used one and our wines turn out just fine.

But if you are curious or want to add some scientific rigor to the process, by all means try one. The instructions can be a bit complicated but basically you are taking a sample of the wine and measuring the amount of sugar that it contains. Above all, remember to do the "before" reading, and to sterilize all pieces of equipment before taking measurements.

racking off

1

2

1. Place the full jug on something so that it sits higher than the second one. Fit one end of the plastc tubing over the top of the racking cane. Place the tip of the racking cane at the bottom of the full vessel; the open end will protrude from the neck. The tip of the racking cane is designed to keep the lees from getting sucked up into the tube.

2. There is more than one way to siphon wine; pictured here is an auto-siphon. To start the suction, give one good pull up and a strong push down on the siphon (you may need another pull-push to get a good flow going). Once the juice is moving, just leave it alone and go with the flow!

3. When most of the juice has moved into the second container, you can tip the original one a bit to draw out as much precious mead or wine as possible, while avoiding the lees.

4. Every time you rack into a clean container, the emptied one must be thoroughly cleaned and sanitized, along with the racking equipment. Discard or compost the dregs.

5. Here you can see the difference between freshly racked wine (at left) and a day or two later, when the solids have settled out.

time to bottle

ONE WAY TO TELL if a still wine really is done fermenting is to move the jug or carboy to a warm spot — 80°F or so — for a few days. If there's any remaining yeast, the wine will reactivate and show bubbles. In that case, wait a while longer to bottle.

Unlike water-bath canning, which requires tempered mason jars, wines can go into any recycled wine or beer bottle and then get a new cap or cork. Red wines must go into dark-colored bottles to prevent the rich color from fading: try green or brown glass bottles. Flower or herb wines look pretty in clear bottles, and fruit wines can go into just about anything. We generally use recycled 1-liter beer bottles or empty 750-milliliter wine bottles.

Beer bottles are capped with metal lids that have a crimped edge. Home brew supply stores sell the caps, along with an inexpensive capping device (around $20). Sanitize the caps before using them. If you use wine bottles, buy corks in bulk, soak them in sanitized water according to directions, and use a hand-powered corker device (starts at $35).

bottling sparkling wines

It's very important to differentiate between still wines, in which all fermentation has stopped, and sparkling wines, which continue to ferment in the bottle.

Still wines pose no risk of exploding in the bottle, but sparkling wines, which typically have sugar added right before bottling, must be in bottles sturdy enough to withstand greater pressure as they age.

The rule of thumb is to add two heaping tablespoons of priming sugar per gallon of wine to the carboy, after the last racking and right before you bottle. Priming sugar differs from regular granulated cane sugar in that it is derived from corn. It is more completely digested by the yeast than other types of sugar, thus creating the most effervescence.

IT'S FINE TO RECYCLE bottles for your fermented beverages, as long as you use only beer bottles for sparkling wines. Regular wine bottles cannot withstand the carbonation pressure.

When you bottle effervescent wine you must use thick Champagne-style bottles with matching corks and bottle wires rather than regular wine bottles. Or you can use beer bottles with crimped caps, which are designed to handle carbonation pressure. Our suggestion? It's easiest to use beer bottles and be done with it. We've never had a mishap.

before you begin

Sanitation is just as important in bottling and later storage as it is in all other parts of the process. Whether you are recycling commercial wine bottles (with new corks) or you've invested in new, perhaps fancier, bottles, you have to clean them all just before you bottle, first by washing them in hot soapy water and then rinsing them well. To sterilize them, use one of the methods suggested below.

Dishwasher. Run the bottles through the dishwasher, using the heated drying cycle. If you can, leave them inside the machine until needed. If not, cover the openings with a clean dishtowel or tinfoil stoppers.

Sanitizer. Fill a clean sink with Star San solution per the instructions on the bottle, or with hot water and add a tablespoon of household bleach. Submerge the bottles and let them soak for 20 minutes. Use canning tongs to remove the bottles, and let them dry upside down in a sterilized drain rack until needed.

Heat. Carefully stack washed bottles in a cold oven, then turn on the oven and heat the bottles using the following guidelines:

Temperature*	Time (Regular/Convection)
340°F (170°C)	60 minutes/45 minutes
320°F (160°C)	120 minutes/90 minutes
285°F (140°C)	180 minutes/140 minutes

Start timing from the point when the sterilizing temperature is reached, not from when the oven is first turned on.

labeling and storage

Just as with canned juices, it is important to label wines, meads, and ciders. Once beverages go into the bottle, especially with dark glass, it's next to impossible to remember what's inside and when you made it. In addition to the name of the wine and the date bottled, you might want to add a list of all the ingredients and the date you actually started fermenting the batch.

Store your filled bottles in a dark place with a cool, stable temperature (about 65°F is ideal). An interior closet or cupboard is perfect, or a dry cellar. Bottles with caps may be stored upright, while those with well-fitting corks may be stored on their side.

bottling

1. One bottling method uses a five-gallon plastic pail with a tap at the bottom. A few days before bottling, strain the finished wine into the sanitized pail. Let the wine sit a day or two to allow remaining sediments to sink to the bottom. Then fill the sanitized bottles directly from the tap which sits above any sediment.

2. We prefer to siphon the wine from the carboy or jug directly into the bottles, using our siphon or racking cane and tubing with a bottle filler attachment. The bottle filler fits on the lower end of the tubing and has a spring-operated stopcock so you don't overfill the bottles. With this method the bottom of the carboy must be higher than the top of the bottle; with the setup shown, you'd have to lower the last bottles a few inches to allow the remaining liquid to flow into them. For sparkling wines, rack one last time into a clean carboy, and add priming sugar before bottling.

3. Once the bottles are filled and corked or capped, wipe them off with water and a bit of bleach or with a bit of sanitizing solution.

TROUBLESHOOTING GUIDE
FOR FERMENTATION

ALL SORTS OF THINGS can go wrong with fermented beverages, but unlike in canning, where some forms of contamination are invisible, with fermentation you can quickly tell when there's a problem: a moldy or cracked cork, an off or bad taste, the unpleasant appearance of a bacterial infection on the must. However, if you practice careful sanitation every step of the way in making your juices and in fermentation, you eliminate most potential problems.

We do want to mention some of the more likely scenarios, how to recognize them, and how to treat them. Winemaking is so easy and generally foolproof that you probably won't have the same difficulties twice.

FERMENTATION DOESN'T BEGIN
Incorrect temperature is a leading suspect. The problem may be a slight case of thermal shock, caused by adding the activated yeast to a must that is too warm or too cool. Temperatures over 104°F kill yeast, while temperatures below 60°F make yeast go dormant. We use the word "lukewarm" throughout our recipes, by which we mean "baby temperature," or a slightly warm feel that wouldn't hurt the tender skin of an infant.

If you suspect the must is too cold, move the fermentation vessel to a warmer place and see if fermentation starts in a few days. If you have to wear a sweater to stay warm in the room, it's too cold. You may also wrap the jug in a layer of blanket or toweling to protect it from the cold.

If fermentation simply hasn't begun after a day or so, or if you suspect you killed the yeast with too much heat, activate another packet of yeast, pitch it in the fermentation vessel, and give it a good shake or swirl. Leave the stopper and airlock off (but cover the mouth with cheesecloth) until you are sure fermentation is well under way.

Another problem might be the yeast itself. Yeast that is past its sell-by date may not be effective. This problem is easily prevented by always using fresh yeast.

FERMENTATION IS STUCK
Your wine, mead, or cider is bubbling along nicely when suddenly the must goes still and there's no more *blurp-blurp-blurp* of carbon dioxide escaping the airlock. Instead of getting weeks or even months of fermentation, you get just a few days. Several problems can cause stuck fermentation, in no particular order or likeliness to occur.

There can be a buildup of carbon dioxide, in which case remove the airlock and stopper, and gently swirl the fermentation vessel to release the buildup. Clean and replace the airlock and see if fermentation resumes.

The problem could be a low level of yeast nutrient. In that case remove the airlock and stopper, drop in a quarter cup of grape skins or raisins, and replace the airlock and stopper. It could also be too little sugar. You can try adding about a cup of sugar per gallon of must, either by pouring the granulated sugar in using a sterilized large funnel, or, if there's room in the carboy, dissolving the sugar in a cup or two of hot water, cooled to lukewarm before adding.

Stuck fermentation can also be a sign of incorrect temperature. If your vessel is too cold the yeast might stop working, and if the vessel has gotten overheated the yeast may be dead. Either bring the jug back up closer to 70°F and watch for signs of life, or in the case of too much heat it may be necessary to activate some new yeast, pitch it in, and put the jug in a cooler place.

WINE DARKENS OR GROWS MOLD

A wine that grows darker and darker is in some trouble, and may be developing an off taste.

You may have used reactive bowls or utensils. Zinc, aluminum, or copper instruments can cause wine to darken; make sure that all of your utensils are made of stainless steel.

Darkness and mold in wine may also be caused by using fruit that was already beginning to rot or that wasn't washed well enough. Mold spores on fruit skins can cause problems.

WINE DEVELOPS HAZY SHEEN, VISCOUS ROPES, OR FLOATERS

These three problems point to bacterial contamination, and the names are perfectly descriptive. If you feel like bailing out on the wine at this point, go ahead. But read on to see what may be happening. In all our winemaking experimentation, the only time we had any problem this serious was when we decided not to add extra yeast for making Peerless Perry. It was an experiment, and now we know.

With a "hazy sheen," the surface of the fermenting liquid is shiny yet hazy at the same time, like a glaze rather than a flat, clear color. The must may contain fruit that was starting to rot when you made the batch. You can try sanitizing the contents with several crushed Campden tablets per gallon and letting it continue fermenting.

The "viscous ropes" are bacteria that take an unpleasant form as they clump throughout the must; such bacteria are ubiquitous. You can try aerating the must by pouring it into a sanitized pail and stirring, then letting solids settle out before pouring the must into a *very* clean fermentation vessel and replacing the airlock.

Finally, "floaters" indicate a usually fatal bacterial condition (fatal for the wine, that is) caused by too much oxygen in the fermentation vessel — in other words, too much space between the liquid and the mouth of the jug or carboy. Bacteria have formed long thin strands. This is where wine turns to vinegar, and not always the gourmet kind. Once this transformation is under way, it is difficult to stop. Dispose of the contents and keep any unsanitized equipment away from other winemaking activities. The rogue bacteria could infect other wines that are undergoing fermentation.

If you have to discard a batch, do an especially thorough job washing and sanitizing your equipment, jugs, and carboys afterward. And buck up! Mistakes in fermentation may break your heart just a little, but they won't break the bank.

Folk wine master

M. A. Jagendorf once wrote,
"Anything that grows
can be turned into a wine."
Are you ready for honeysuckle
wine or grape leaf wine?

wines, meads & specialty drinks

easy garden grape wine

INGREDIENTS

- 2 quarts filtered water, plus 2 cups
- 2 quarts Big Wow Grape Cider (page 78) or other pure grape juice
- 2 teaspoons (1 packet) Pasteur Champagne yeast or white or red wine yeast
- 4 cups sugar
- 1 cup grape skins left over from pressing, or ½ cup raisins (not golden)
- 2 heaping tablespoons priming sugar (optional)

YES, HOMEMADE GRAPE WINE can be sweet. If you prefer to drink dry Spanish-style wine or nothing, well, this recipe may not be for you. But for the sheer satisfaction of an easy start-to-finish winemaking experience, garden grapes can't be beat.

Grapes of one kind or another grow all over North America, in every climate and topography. In the South, the local naturalized grapes include the muscadine (purple skins) and the scuppernong (green skins). The skins are thick, and the individual grapes quite large. Plus they are juicy and filled with sugar. The deep sugar base helps make fermentation nearly foolproof.

If you have access to a fruit press with a grinder attachment, you can start your Garden Grape Wine in early autumn, bottle it in winter, and have a treat for the following holiday season.

Dee-licious! This is a rosé with class.

Makes approximately 1 gallon

PREP TIME: About a ½ hour, plus time for fermenting and bottling

1. Bring the 2 quarts and 2 cups of filtered water to a boil in a large pot.

2. Heat 1 cup of the Big Wow Grape Cider or grape juice to lukewarm (approximately 100–105°F), and sprinkle with the yeast. Set the mixture aside to let it proof.

3. Pour the sugar into a sterilized 1-gallon fermentation jug.

4. Transfer 2 cups of the boiling water into the jug, and swirl or shake it until sugar is dissolved. Remove the remaining water from the heat.

5. Add the remaining grape juice to the jug.

6. Add the grape skins or raisins.

7. Add enough of the remaining heated water to fill the jug to the shoulders, leaving enough room to add the yeast mixture.

8. Allow the mixture in the jug to cool; when it is lukewarm (100–105°F), add the proofed yeast mixture.

9. Stopper the jug with a sterilized airlock, and check in 1 hour to make sure the airlock is bubbling.

10. Set the jug in a cool, dark place until the bubbling stops and the liquid clears. This fermentation can take 2 weeks to several months. Don't be concerned about how the mixture looks after a few weeks, as it may darken during fermentation. If the bubbling stops unexpectedly, see the Troubleshooting Guide for Fermentation (page 128).

11. Rack the wine. (This may be repeated several times until the wine has cleared.)

12. Bottle the wine, and let it age for at least 1 year.

Optional: **MAKE IT SPARKLE!**

- To create an effervescent wine, rack the wine into a clean jug.
- Dissolve 2 heaping tablespoons of priming sugar in a small amount of warm water, and add to the jug.
- Swirl the wine to distribute the dissolved sugar and bottle immediately.

Cook's Tip

Where to begin with grapes? For maximum juice, look to wine grape vines rather than table grape varieties. Many kinds of grapes may not be shipped legally to a number of states, where commercial wineries could be hurt by disease outbreaks. Here are a few varieties with no restrictions: Müller-Thurgau (light green grapes), Pinot Gris (for white wine), Concord (robust reds), Buffalo (like Concord), and Aurore (gold to pink grapes).

all-around herb wine

INGREDIENTS

- 1 gallon filtered water, plus 2 cups
- 2 quarts fresh herbs (2 wide-mouth quart canning jars lightly packed with leaves or flowers)
- 1 cup of any fruit juice
- 2 teaspoons (1 packet) Pasteur Champagne yeast or white wine yeast
- 1 inch fresh ginger, cut into slices
- 4 cups sugar
- ½ organic orange with peel, chopped
- ½ cup raisins (not golden)
- 1 thick slice (about 1 inch) organic lemon with peel, chopped
- 2 heaping tablespoons of priming sugar (optional)

HERB WINES MAKE GOOD USE of the most prolific — sometimes pesky — plants in the garden. The kinds of herb wine you make will depend on where in the country you live and what plants your local conditions favor. Choices may include anise, hyssop, lemon balm, dill, fennel, nettle, raspberry leaf, chickweed, rose petal, or cilantro.

Think of herb wines as health drinks from the past. The flavors can be delicate and entrancing, or distinctive and refreshing. Small bottles of your homemade herb wines make fantastic gifts for friends. Herb wines age gracefully. It's easy to get addicted to this hobby, so get ready to stock your wine closet or basement with products that will only get better with the passage of time.

When measuring fresh herbs, it may be necessary to start with twice the amount called for, because stems and damaged leaves must be discarded. You can substitute dried herbs with equal success, but use different proportions: 3 to 4 ounces total dry weight instead of 2 quarts fresh material.

Makes approximately 1 gallon

PREP TIME: About 1 hour, plus time for fermenting and bottling

1. **Bring the gallon** of water to a boil in a large pot, for cooking the ginger. At the same time, place the 2 cups of water in a kettle and bring to a boil.

2. **Rinse the herbs,** removing the stems, and set aside.

3. **Heat the juice** to lukewarm (approximately 100–105°F), and sprinkle with the yeast. Set the mixture aside to let it proof.

4. **Add the ginger** to the large pot of boiling water and boil gently, uncovered, for 5–10 minutes. The longer the ginger cooks, the more pronounced the flavor.

5. **Add the herbs** to the boiling ginger-and-water mixture, remove from the heat, cover, and steep for at least 10 minutes but no more than 1 hour, to make a strong tea.

6. **Pour the sugar** into a sterilized 1-gallon fermentation jug.

7. **Pour the 2 cups** of boiling water into the jug, and swirl or shake it until the sugar is dissolved.

8. **Put the chopped** orange, raisins, and lemon slice into the jug.

9. **Strain the herb** tea into the jug, leaving enough room to add the yeast mixture.

10. **Allow the mixture** to cool; when it is lukewarm (100–105°F), add the proofed yeast mixture.

11. **Stopper the jug** with a sterilized airlock, and check in 1 hour to make sure the airlock is bubbling.

12. **Set the jug** in a cool, dark place until the bubbling stops and the liquid clears. This fermentation can take 2 weeks to several months. Don't be concerned about how the mixture looks, as it may darken during fermentation. If the bubbling stops unexpectedly, see the Troubleshooting Guide for Fermentation (page 128).

13. **Rack the wine.** (This may be repeated several times until the wine has cleared.)

14. **Bottle the wine,** and let it age for 6 months to 1 year.

Optional: **MAKE IT SPARKLE!**

- To create an effervescent wine, rack the wine into a clean jug.

- Dissolve 2 heaping tablespoons of priming sugar in a small amount of warm water, and add to the jug.

- Swirl the wine to distribute the dissolved sugar and bottle immediately.

Cook's Tip

Don't be afraid to use different herb combinations or even add fruit or spices to the mix. These combinations can make excellent beverages.

dandelion wine

THE BEST DANDELION WINE is like bottled sunshine: light, bright, and happy. Once called poor man's wine, it was a favorite of early American pioneers as they made their way across the country and settled down.

This is a beverage made in spring as lawns everywhere sprout countless yellow dandelion blossoms that begged to be picked. Be sure to take them from a lawn that hasn't been sprayed with pesticides or herbicides. Then take care that all of the bitter green stems and sepals are removed. You want only the flower petals. This is a pleasant family activity: let the smallest tykes help out, and the work goes fast.

Plan ahead, for the flowers quickly wilt and lose their appeal. Your product will be the very best if you can take the petals directly from outdoors to the kitchen and start cooking. Make the tea immediately. With its straw-yellow color, dandelion wine makes a nice afternoon spritzer and can be cut with club soda or another carbonated mixer.

Makes approximately 1 gallon

PREP TIME: About 1 hour, plus 24–48 hours for steeping, plus time for fermenting and bottling

INGREDIENTS

- 1 gallon filtered water, plus 2 cups
- 2 quarts fresh dandelion flowers, with the stems and sepals removed
- 1 cup of any fruit juice
- 2 teaspoons (1 packet) Pasteur Champagne yeast or white wine yeast
- 4 cups sugar
- ½ cup raisins (not golden)
- 2 inches fresh ginger, cut into slices
- 1 organic lemon, chopped, with the peel
- 2 heaping tablespoons priming sugar (optional)

1. Bring the gallon of water to a boil in a large pot and add the dandelion flowers. Immediately remove from the heat, cover, and let stand 24 to 48 hours. Dandelion flavor is a delicate thing. Let this tea sit as long as possible to intensify the flavor.

2. After the dandelion tea has steeped, place the 2 cups of filtered water in a kettle and bring to a boil.

3. Heat the juice to lukewarm (approximately 100–105°F), and sprinkle with the yeast. Set the mixture aside to let it proof.

4. Pour the sugar into a sterilized 1-gallon fermentation jug.

5. Pour the 2 cups of boiling water into the jug, and swirl or shake it until sugar is dissolved. Add the raisins, ginger, and chopped lemon to the jug.

6. Strain the dandelion tea into the jug, squeezing the herb mixture to extract as much liquid as possible. Fill the jug to the shoulders, leaving enough room to add the yeast mixture.

7. Allow the mixture to cool; when it is lukewarm (100–105°F), add the proofed yeast mixture.

8. Stopper the jug with a sterilized airlock, and check in 1 hour to make sure the airlock is bubbling.

9. Set the jug in a cool, dark place until the bubbling stops and the liquid clears. This fermentation can take 2 weeks to several months. Don't be concerned about how the mixture looks after a few weeks, as it may darken during fermentation. If the bubbling stops unexpectedly, see the Troubleshooting Guide for Fermentation (page 128).

10. Rack the wine. (This may be repeated several times until wine has cleared.)

11. Bottle the wine, and let it age for 6 months to 1 year. The flavor may improve over a second year.

Optional: **MAKE IT SPARKLE!**

- To create an effervescent wine, rack the wine into a clean jug.

- Dissolve 2 heaping tablespoons of priming sugar in a small amount of warm water, and add to the jug.

- Swirl the wine to distribute the dissolved sugar and bottle immediately.

garden mint wine

INGREDIENTS

- 1 gallon filtered water
- 1 cup of orange juice
- 2 teaspoons (1 packet) Pasteur Champagne yeast or white wine yeast
- 4 cups sugar
- 2 quarts fresh mint leaves, washed
- 2 heaping tablespoons priming sugar (optional)

SURPRISE! Garden Mint Wine doesn't taste sweet or syrupy, as you might expect, but is light and only slightly minty. It's also crystal-clear and ever so slightly effervescent, and serves up like Vinho Verde. You can make Garden Mint Wine at any time of year when the mint isn't blooming, but the flavor will be at its best in late spring, before summer's heat has removed some of the flavorful essential oils from the leaves. Pick double the amount of mint leaves called for in the recipe, because the stalks and any damaged leaves must be discarded.

Of course you can use any fruit juice to proof the yeast, but we have found here that citrus juice best balances with the mint. Age this wine six months to a year, to let the flavor mellow.

Makes approximately 1 gallon

PREP TIME: About 1 hour, plus time for fermenting and bottling

1. Bring the gallon of filtered water to a boil in a large pot.

2. Heat the orange juice to lukewarm (approximately 100–105°F), and sprinkle with the yeast. Set the mixture aside to let it proof.

3. Pour the sugar into a sterilized 1-gallon fermentation jug.

4. Pour 2 cups of the boiling water into the jug, and swirl or shake it until sugar is dissolved.

5. Add the mint leaves, stuffing them into the jug with a long utensil if necessary, and enough additional boiling water to fill the jug to the shoulders, leaving enough room to add the yeast mixture.

6. Allow the mixture to cool; when it is lukewarm (100–105°F), add the proofed yeast mixture.

7. Stopper the jug with a sterilized air-lock, and check in 1 hour to make sure the airlock is bubbling.

8. Set the jug in a cool, dark place until the bubbling stops and the liquid clears. This fermentation can take 2 weeks to several months. Don't be concerned about how the mixture looks after a few weeks, as it may darken during fermentation. If the bubbling stops unexpectedly, see the Troubleshooting Guide for Fermentation (page 128).

9. Rack the wine. (This may be repeated several times until wine has cleared.)

10. Bottle the wine, and let it age for 6 months to 1 year.

Optional: **MAKE IT SPARKLE!**

- To create an effervescent wine, rack the wine into a clean jug.

- Dissolve 2 heaping tablespoons of priming sugar in a small amount of warm water, and add to the jug.

- Swirl the wine to distribute the dissolved sugar and bottle immediately.

Cook's Tip

This recipe works best with mild mints such as spearmint, apple mint, or regular garden mint. Avoid strong mint varieties such as chocolate mint or peppermint; wines made from these taste more like medicine than something to drink with dinner.

To intensify the mint flavor, add half a teaspoon of Mint Syrup (page 183) to each glass when serving the finished wine.

parsley wine

ACCORDING TO FOLK WISDOM, parsley wine is helpful for treating arthritis. Goodness knows that gardeners can get sore joints after years of work.

If your garden conditions favor parsley, or you have an abundant source of organic parsley from a local farm, try parsley wine for its surprisingly sweet, light flavor. It does not matter what type of parsley is used. We tested this recipe with a combination of both flat-leaf and curly parsley. The result was very mild and quite tasty. In this recipe we proofed the yeast with jelly dissolved in water, just to show you can improvise according to what's on hand.

The time-consuming part of this recipe is trimming the thicker stalks from the parsley, leaving mostly the nutritious leaves and short stalks for the brew.

Makes approximately 1 gallon

PREP TIME: About 1 hour, plus 8–12 hours for steeping, plus time for fermenting and bottling

INGREDIENTS

1 gallon filtered water, plus 3 cups

2 quarts parsley leaves, trimmed of large stems

1 cup chopped raisins (not golden)

1 tablespoon any jelly or preserves mixed with enough water to make 1 cup

2 teaspoons (1 packet) Pasteur Champagne yeast or yeast for white wine

4 cups sugar

2 organic lemons, chopped, including the peel

2 heaping tablespoons priming sugar (optional)

1. Bring the gallon of water to a boil in a large pot, add the parsley and raisins, immediately remove from the heat, cover, and let stand 8–12 hours or overnight to make a strong tea.

2. After the parsley tea has steeped, place 2 cups of the water in a kettle and bring to a boil.

3. Heat the jelly-water mixture to lukewarm (approximately 100–105°F), and sprinkle with the yeast. Set the mixture aside to let it proof.

4. Pour the sugar into a sterilized 1-gallon fermentation jug.

5. Pour the 2 cups of boiling water into the jug, and swirl or shake it until the sugar is dissolved.

6. Add the chopped lemons.

7. Strain the tea into the jug, squeezing the parsley-raisin mixture to extract as much liquid as possible. Fill the jug to the shoulders, leaving enough room to add the yeast mixture.

8. Add the proofed yeast to the slightly warm contents of the carboy.

9. Stopper the jug with a sterilized air-lock, and check in 1 hour to make sure the airlock is bubbling.

10. Set the jug in a cool, dark place until the bubbling stops and the liquid clears. This fermentation can take 2 weeks to several months. Don't be concerned about how the mixture looks after a few weeks, as it may darken during fermentation. If the bubbling stops unexpectedly, see the Troubleshooting Guide for Fermentation (page 128).

11. Rack the wine. (This may be repeated several times until wine has cleared.)

12. Bottle the wine, and let it age for at least 6 months. The wine improves after 1 year or more.

Optional: **MAKE IT SPARKLE!**

- To create an effervescent wine, rack the wine into a clean jug.

- Dissolve 2 heaping tablespoons of priming sugar in a small amount of warm water, and add to the jug.

- Swirl the wine to distribute the dissolved sugar and bottle immediately.

passion-flower–lemon balm wine

INGREDIENTS

- 1 gallon filtered water, plus 2 cups
- 1 cup any fruit juice
- 2 teaspoons (1 packet) Pasteur Champagne yeast or white wine yeast
- 2 ounces of dried passionflower, leaves and flowers
- 1 ounce dried lemon balm, leaves and flowers
- 1 inch fresh ginger, cut into slices
- 4 cups sugar
- ½ cup raisins (not golden)
- 1 organic lemon and ½ organic orange, chopped, including the peel
- 2 heaping tablespoons priming sugar (optional)

BOUQUET: APRICOT. Color: spun gold. Flavor: like melon liqueur. The secret of this stellar wine lies in the passionflower, a bewitching vine with outlandish floral patterns. This recipe uses the whole plant except for the roots.

There's one great challenge in making this wine: Passionflower doesn't necessarily mature at the same time as lemon balm. Make this wine in the spring by using fresh lemon balm and dried passionflower from the previous year; or make it in the fall using fresh passionflower and dried lemon balm from the past spring. We have made it with all the herbs dried, and the result was outstanding. Any of these methods produces equally good, though slightly different, results.

This wine is well worth the time and effort. Plan ahead in order to harvest and dry the main herbal ingredients at their peak.

Makes approximately 1 gallon

PREP TIME: About 1 hour, plus time for fermenting and bottling

1. Bring the gallon of water to a boil in a large pot. At the same time, place the 2 cups of water in a kettle and bring to a boil.

2. Heat the juice to lukewarm (approximately 100–105°F), and sprinkle with the yeast. Set the mixture aside to let it proof.

3. Add the dried herbs and ginger to the pot and boil gently, uncovered, about 5–10 minutes.

4. Remove from the heat, cover, and steep for at least 10 minutes but no more than 1 hour, to make a strong tea. Strain and set aside.

5. Pour the sugar into a sterilized 1-gallon fermentation jug.

6. Pour the 2 cups of boiling water from the kettle into the jug, and swirl or shake it until sugar is dissolved.

7. Add the raisins, lemon, and orange to the jug.

8. Pour the herb tea into the jug, filling it to the shoulders leaving enough room to add the yeast mixture.

9. Allow the mixture to cool; when it is lukewarm (100–105°F), add the proofed yeast mixture.

10. Stopper the jug with a sterilized airlock, and check in 1 hour to make sure the airlock is bubbling.

11. Set the jug in a cool, dark place until the bubbling stops and the liquid clears. This fermentation can take 2 weeks to several months. Don't be concerned about how the mixture looks after a few weeks, as it may darken during fermentation. If the bubbling stops unexpectedly, see the Troubleshooting Guide for Fermentation (page 128).

12. Rack the wine. (This may be repeated several times until wine has cleared.)

13. Bottle the wine, and let it age for at least 6 months. The wine improves after 1 year or more.

Optional: **MAKE IT SPARKLE!**

- To create an effervescent wine, rack the wine into a clean jug.

- Dissolve 2 heaping tablespoons of priming sugar in a small amount of warm water, and add to the jug.

- Swirl the wine to distribute the dissolved sugar and bottle immediately.

Cook's Tip

You can add or intensify flavor in Passionflower–Lemon Balm Wine by adding fruit juice, syrup, or additional herb tea to the wine after it has been racked and before it is bottled.

heirloom potato wine

AMERICANS LOVE POTATOES, and American gardeners are discovering just how easy and rewarding it is to grow their potatoes at home rather than relying on factory-farmed produce. Varieties abound, with potatoes ripening in a rainbow of colors (red, white, and even blue) and in lots of sizes and shapes. Look for heirloom seed potatoes from your own region for a satisfying harvest.

Old World wine master M. A. Jagendorf described potato wine as having a higher alcohol content than most wines, with a distinctive hearty flavor. He suggests using a little bruised ginger to modify the taste. You can experiment with different kinds of potatoes in this recipe.

The flavor of the wine going into the bottle is surprisingly sweet; it's delicious and exciting, with earthy undertones. We used purple heirloom potatoes to test this recipe, giving the finished product a lovely rose cast. As the wine ages, the bold flavor characteristics of the potatoes comes through, but in a pleasant way, and this wine almost tastes like a mild vodka.

Makes approximately 1 gallon

PREP TIME: About 1 hour, plus time for fermenting and bottling

INGREDIENTS

- 1 gallon filtered water
- 1 cup any fruit juice
- 2 teaspoons (1 packet) Pasteur Champagne yeast or white wine yeast
- 4 cups sugar
- 3 medium or 4 small potatoes (about 1 pound), unpeeled but with bad spots removed, chopped small enough to fit through the neck of the jug
- ½ cup raisins (not golden)
- 2 heaping tablespoons priming sugar (optional)

1. Bring the water to a boil in a large pot.

2. Heat the juice to lukewarm (approximately 100–105°F), and sprinkle with the yeast. Set the mixture aside to let it proof.

3. Pour the sugar into a sterilized 1-gallon fermentation jug.

4. Transfer 2 cups of the boiling water into the jug, and swirl or shake it until the sugar is dissolved.

5. Add the potatoes and raisins. Add enough of the remaining boiled water to fill the jug to the shoulders, leaving enough room to add the yeast mixture.

6. Allow the mixture to cool; when it is lukewarm (100–105°F), add the proofed yeast mixture.

7. Stopper the jug with a sterilized airlock, and check in 1 hour to make sure the airlock is bubbling.

8. Set the jug in a cool, dark place until the bubbling stops and the liquid clears. This fermentation can take 2 weeks to several months. Don't be concerned about how the mixture looks after a few weeks, as it may darken during fermentation. If the bubbling stops unexpectedly, see the Troubleshooting Guide for Fermentation (page 128).

9. Rack the wine. (This may be repeated several times until wine has cleared.)

10. Bottle the wine, and let it age for 6 months to 1 year. The flavor may improve over time.

Optional: MAKE IT SPARKLE!

- To create an effervescent wine, rack the wine into a clean jug.

- Dissolve 2 heaping tablespoons of priming sugar in a small amount of warm water, and add to the jug.

- Swirl the wine to distribute the dissolved sugar and bottle immediately.

prickly pear cactus wine

WELL, WHY NOT? Prickly pear cactus, which you may find roaming wild over neglected real estate, can produce gallons of ripe fruit in the fall. The starting point for wine is to turn a few pounds of the bright red tunas into juice, straining it carefully of course. From there, the process is the same as for other fruit wines.

As it matures, this unusual wine tastes sweet but with citrus notes at the end, as wine critics say. We love it and think you will, too!

Makes approximately 1 gallon

PREP TIME: About a ½ hour, plus time for fermenting and bottling

INGREDIENTS

- 2 cups filtered water
- 4 quarts Prickly Pear Cactus Juice (page 90)
- 2 teaspoons (1 packet) Montrachet or other red wine yeast
- 4 cups sugar
- ½ cup raisins (not golden) or ¼ cup grape skins left over from pressing grapes
- 2 heaping tablespoons priming sugar (optional)

1. Bring the water to a boil in a kettle.

2. Heat 1 cup of Prickly Pear Cactus Juice to lukewarm (approximately 100–105°F), and sprinkle with the yeast. Set the mixture aside to let it proof.

3. Pour the sugar into a sterilized 1-gallon fermentation jug.

4. Pour the 2 cups of boiling water from the kettle into the jug, and swirl or shake it until sugar is dissolved.

5. Add the raisins or grape skins.

6. Add the remaining Prickly Pear Cactus Juice. Fill the jug to the shoulders with boiled water, leaving enough room to add the yeast mixture.

7. Allow the mixture to cool; when it is lukewarm (100–105°F), add the proofed yeast mixture.

8. Stopper the jug with a sterilized airlock, and check in 1 hour to make sure the airlock is bubbling.

9. Set the jug in a cool, dark place until the bubbling stops and the liquid clears. This fermentation can take 2 weeks to several months. If the bubbling stops unexpectedly, see the Troubleshooting Guide for Fermentation (page 128).

10. Rack the wine. (This may be repeated several times until wine has cleared.)

11. Bottle the wine, and let it age for at least 1 year.

Optional: MAKE IT SPARKLE!

- To create an effervescent wine, rack the wine into a clean jug.

- Dissolve 2 heaping tablespoons of priming sugar in a small amount of warm water, and add to the jug.

- Swirl the wine to distribute the dissolved sugar and bottle immediately.

Cook's Tip

Use leftover Prickly Pear Cactus Juice (page 90) for topping up this wine when you rack it. You can use it to proof the yeast for other wine or mead recipes to impart a beautiful pink hue to your brew.

bitchin' birch wine

INGREDIENTS

- 2 **cups filtered water**
- ½ **cup any fruit juice**
- 2 **teaspoons (1 packet) dry wine yeast**
- 4 **cups sugar**
- 1 **teaspoon commercial yeast nutrient or ½ cup raisins (not golden)**
- 4 **quarts birch sap**
- 2 **heaping tablespoons priming sugar (optional)**

YOU MAY NOT REALIZE that you have a wine tree in your yard, but if there's a mature birch nearby, the raw material, birch sap, is right at hand if you want to tap into it. Or it might be easier to look for a Slavic grocery store; we stumbled across a 1-gallon jar of Russian birch water (that's sap) for sale at a local Russian goods store and decided to experiment.

Forget about the image of thick, sticky sap. Birch sap really is like water: it's thin and almost clear, but flavored with a mysterious essence of the forest, a bit mossy with floral hints. The difference between birch wine and birch beer? Birch beer is a nonalcoholic beverage made from root and bark extracts, similar to root beer, while birch wine is fermented from birch sap.

That gallon of store-bought birch sap was the basis for this recipe. The finished product is bright and slightly sweet, very pleasant to drink. In fact, we'll go ahead and call it a health drink, a light treat in spring or summer.

Makes approximately 1 gallon

PREP TIME: About a ½ hour, plus time for fermenting and bottling

1. Bring the water to a boil. At the same time, heat the juice to lukewarm (approximately 100–105°F), and sprinkle with the yeast. Set the mixture aside to proof.

2. Pour the sugar into a sterilized 1-gallon fermentation jug.

3. Pour the boiling water into the jug, and swirl or shake it until sugar is dissolved.

4. Add the commercial yeast nutrient or raisins.

5. Fill the jug to the shoulders with the birch sap, leaving enough room to add the yeast mixture.

6. Allow the mixture to cool; when it is lukewarm (100–105°F), add the proofed yeast mixture.

7. Stopper the jug with a sterilized airlock, and check in 1 hour to make sure the airlock is bubbling.

8. Set the jug in a cool, dark place until the bubbling stops and the liquid clears. This fermentation can take 2 weeks to several months. If the bubbling stops unexpectedly, see the Troubleshooting Guide for Fermentation (page 128).

9. Rack the wine. (This may be repeated several times until wine has cleared.)

10. Bottle the wine, and let it age for 6 months to 1 year or more.

Optional: MAKE IT SPARKLE!

- To create an effervescent wine, rack the wine into a clean jug.

- Dissolve 2 heaping tablespoons of priming sugar in a small amount of warm water, and add to the jug.

- Swirl the wine to distribute the dissolved sugar and bottle immediately.

Cook's Tip

To preserve the delicate flavor of the birch water, we reduced the usual amount of fruit juice and used a commercial yeast nutrient instead of raisins. This nutrient does not influence the wine's flavor but does provide nitrogen for proper fermentation. To retain the most birch flavor, heat 2 cups of the birch sap instead of filtered water to melt the sugar in the jug when preparing the wine.

basic mead

INGREDIENTS

- 1 gallon filtered water
- 1 quart raw honey by volume (about 3 pounds)
- 1 cup any fruit juice or 1–2 tablespoons any jelly dissolved in 1 cup of filtered water
- 2 teaspoons (1 packet) Pasteur Champagne yeast or yeast for white wine
- ½ cup raisins (not golden)
- 2 heaping tablespoons per gallon priming sugar (optional)

MEAD IS AN ANCIENT BEVERAGE made from honey and water. Mead is versatile and can be flavored by fruits, herbs, or flowers. The only limit is your imagination. Try chocolate mead or hot pepper mead! The taste sensation is rich and complex. No matter what flavor of mead you make, the result can be sublime, making any occasion memorable.

The aroma of honey meets the nose before mead meets the tongue. Then comes a river of sensation: a velvety sweetness, a slight mystery that speaks of time and patience. Mead is not a beverage to quaff at dinner, but rather a treat to savor with close friends or family in front of a fire. Perfect with appetizers, mead is a special drink for special events.

Don't be put off by the price of honey used to make mead. Honey from a local producer may be surprisingly inexpensive, depending on your region, and so a finished batch of mead may cost $1 or less a bottle. The flavorings are also inexpensive when you grow or pick your own.

We recommend against microwaving honey to heat it for our mead recipes. Microwaving honey can alter the flavor, and overheating can "cook out" some of honey's goodness.

Makes approximately 1 gallon

PREP TIME: About 1 hour, plus time for fermenting and bottling

1. **Bring the gallon** of water to a boil in a large pot.

2. **Warm the honey** by placing the jar in a bowl of hot water.

3. **Heat the fruit** juice or jelly and water to lukewarm (approximately 100–105°F), and sprinkle with the yeast. Set the mixture aside to let it proof.

4. **Pour the warm** honey into a sterilized 1-gallon fermentation jug.

5. **Fill the jug** about halfway with the boiled water, and swirl vigorously to mix honey and water.

6. **Add the raisins.**

7. **Fill the jug** to the shoulders with boiled water, leaving enough room to add the yeast mixture.

8. **Allow the mixture** to cool; when it is lukewarm (100–105°F), add the proofed yeast mixture.

9. **Stopper the jug** with a sterilized airlock, and check in 1 hour to make sure the airlock is bubbling.

10. **Set the jug** in a cool, dark place until the bubbling stops and the liquid clears. This fermentation can take 2 weeks to several months. Don't be concerned about how the mixture looks after a few weeks, as it may darken during fermentation. If the bubbling stops unexpectedly, see the Troubleshooting Guide for Fermentation (page 128).

11. **Rack the mead.** (This may be repeated several times until mead has cleared.)

12. **Bottle the mead,** and let it age for at least 6 months. The mead improves after 1 year or more.

Optional: **MAKE IT SPARKLE!**

- To create an effervescent mead, rack the mead into a clean jug.

- Dissolve 2 heaping tablespoons of priming sugar in a small amount of warm water, and add to the jug.

- Swirl the mead to distribute the dissolved sugar and bottle immediately.

Cook's Tip

Some people may be concerned about using raw honey. Most store-bought honey has been pasteurized (heated to 161°F), which kills bacteria but strips the honey of flavor and character. This recipe uses raw honey; in fermentation, the vigorous growth of yeast wins out over the growth of bacteria. If, improbably, yeast growth is weak and bacteria are present, you will be able to tell by a bad smell. In that case, discard the mead immediately and start over.

red, white, and blueberry mead

INGREDIENTS

- 1 gallon filtered water
- 1 quart honey by volume (about 3 pounds)
- 1 cup any fruit juice or 1–2 tablespoons any jelly dissolved in 1 cup of filtered water
- 2 teaspoons (1 packet) of Pasteur Champagne yeast or yeast for white wine
- ½ cup fresh basil leaves, loosely packed
- 2 pints blueberries, divided
- ½ cup crystallized ginger
- 2 heaping tablespoons priming sugar (optional)

THE INSPIRATION behind this mead is the simple and highly pleasurable experience of picking ripe blueberries. Summer, blueberries, and Fourth of July festivities go together naturally, and here's a way to bottle up that special time of year so that you can release it when the weather turns cold. As you sip, you can recall warm, lazy afternoons of picking and munching blueberries.

If you can stand to leave this mead in the bottle for two or three years, it develops a full, mild flavor, with just a knife edge of berries and spice running through it. As it ages, it also changes color slightly, going from a pale golden yellow to the lovely amber of a good beer, with tiny effervescent bubbles rising in the glass.

Note the unusual addition of basil in this recipe, as well as the substitution of crystallized ginger for raisins and the inclusion of a second measure of blueberry tea before bottling.

Makes approximately 1 gallon

PREP TIME: About 1 hour, plus time for fermenting and bottling

1. Bring the water to a boil in a large pot.

2. Warm the honey by placing the jar in a bowl of hot water.

3. Heat the fruit juice or jelly and water to lukewarm (approximately 100–105°F), and sprinkle with the yeast. Set the mixture aside to let it proof.

4. Add the basil and 1 pint of blueberries to the boiling water. Cover, remove from the heat, and let steep at least 10 minutes but no more than 1 hour.

5. Freeze the other pint of blueberries to use when you rack the mead later.

6. Pour the warm honey into a sterilized 1-gallon fermentation jug.

7. Add the crystallized ginger.

8. Add half the basil-blueberry tea, unstrained, to the jug, using a sterilized funnel. Swirl to mix with the honey.

9. Fill the jug to the shoulders with the remaining tea, leaving enough room to add the yeast mixture.

10. Allow the mixture to cool; when it is lukewarm (100–105°F), add the proofed yeast mixture.

11. Stopper the jug with a sterilized airlock, and check in 1 hour to make sure the airlock is bubbling.

12. Set the jug in a cool, dark place until the bubbling stops and the liquid clears. This fermentation can take 2 weeks to several months. Don't be concerned about how the mixture looks after a few weeks, as it may darken during fermentation. If the bubbling stops unexpectedly, see the Troubleshooting Guide for Fermentation (page 128).

13. Rack the mead. (This may be repeated several times until mead has cleared.)

14. During the final rack, make a second tea using the pint of frozen blueberries and 2 cups of boiling water; simmer for 5 minutes, cover, and let cool to room temperature. Strain the tea into the jug.

15. Bottle the mead, and let it age for at least 6 months. The mead improves after 1 year or more.

Optional: MAKE IT SPARKLE!

- To create an effervescent mead, rack the mead into a clean jug.

- Dissolve 2 heaping tablespoons of priming sugar in a small amount of warm water, and add to the jug.

- Swirl the mead to distribute the dissolved sugar and bottle immediately.

Cook's Tip

Try holy basil — also known as tulsi — instead of regular basil to add exotic notes of flavor and spice to the mead. This herb is fun and easy to grow, and features prominently in Thai cuisine. Research has shown tulsi to have strong medicinal properties.

mixed berry mead

INGREDIENTS

- 1 gallon filtered water
- 1 quart honey by volume (about 3 pounds)
- 1 cup any fruit juice or 1–2 tablespoons any jelly dissolved in 1 cup filtered water
- 2 teaspoons (1 packet) of Pasteur Champagne yeast or yeast for white wine
- 1¼ pounds fresh or frozen mixed berries (blueberries, raspberries, strawberries, blackberries, or other berries)
- ½ cup raisins (not golden)
- 2 heaping tablespoons priming sugar (optional)

MIXED BERRY MEAD may have a rosy pink cast, depending on the berry mix: blueberries, raspberries, strawberries, serviceberries, blackberries, or any other kind of berry you find. You will inevitably vary the mixture of fruit from year to year, and the results will vary as well. Be sure to include the ingredients and the year on your labels.

Mixed Berry Mead settles down with age, losing its slight tang and gaining a rich interaction between the sugars. And it is a healthier-choice alcoholic drink, because it preserves the goodness of the honey and the medicinal properties of the berries. All those antioxidants!

TRY THIS MEAD as an ingredient in a holiday punch: it blends well with all sorts of other flavors. In addition, as a mixer for cocktails it's hard to beat.

Makes approximately 1 gallon

PREP TIME: About 1 hour, plus time for fermenting and bottling

1. Bring the water to a boil in a large pot.

2. Warm the honey by placing the jar in a bowl of hot water.

3. Heat the fruit juice or jelly and water to lukewarm (approximately 100–105°F), and sprinkle with the yeast. Set the mixture aside to let it proof.

4. Add 1 pound of the fresh or frozen berries to the boiling filtered water. Lower heat and simmer for 10 minutes. Freeze the remaining berries to use when you rack the mead.

5. Pour the warm honey into a sterilized 1-gallon fermentation jug.

6. Add the raisins.

7. Strain the berry juice to remove the solids.

8. Add about half of the hot juice to the jug, using a sterilized funnel. Swirl to mix with the honey.

9. Fill the rest of the way with the remaining juice, leaving enough room to add the yeast mixture.

10. Allow the mixture to cool; when it is lukewarm (100–105°F), add the proofed yeast mixture.

11. Stopper the jug with a sterilized airlock, and check in 1 hour to make sure the airlock is bubbling.

12. Set the jug in a cool, dark place until the bubbling stops and the liquid clears. This fermentation can take 2 weeks to several months. Don't be concerned about how the mixture looks after a few weeks, as it may darken during fermentation. If the bubbling stops unexpectedly, see the Troubleshooting Guide for Fermentation (page 128).

13. Rack the mead. (This may be repeated several times until mead has cleared.)

14. During the final rack, make a second tea of the remaining berries by adding them to 2 cups of boiling filtered water; simmer for 5 minutes, cover, and let cool to room temperature. Strain this tea into the jug, and swirl it to mix.

15. Bottle the mead, and let it age for at least 6 months. The mead improves after 1 year or more.

Optional: **MAKE IT SPARKLE!**

- To create an effervescent mead, rack the mead into a clean jug.

- Dissolve 2 heaping tablespoons of priming sugar in a small amount of warm water, and add to the jug.

- Swirl the mead to distribute the dissolved sugar and bottle immediately.

old crabby mead

Makes approximately 1 gallon

PREP TIME: About 1 hour, plus time for fermenting and bottling

INGREDIENTS

- 1 quart honey by volume (about 3 pounds)
- 1 cup any fruit juice
- 2 teaspoons (1 packet) Pasteur Champagne yeast or yeast for white wine
- 1 quart Crab Apple Juice (page 80)
- ¼ pound grated fresh ginger
- ½ cup raisins (not golden)
- 2–3 quarts filtered water
- 2 heaping tablespoons priming sugar (optional)

YOU'LL SMELL ROSES as soon as you raise a glass of this lively mead, which packs a punch along with its delicate scent. After all, crab apples are prominent members of the rose family. The right kinds of crab apples produce loads of small but delicious fruit every year. Kerr and Callaway Crab are favorites of ours, although any neighborhood variety may work.

To test for taste, pick a handful, boil them up, strain the liquid, and taste; if the result is bitter, don't use them but if the flavor is just tart or slightly sour, go ahead. Here's a great way to use some of the harvest.

In the bottle, Old Crabby Mead changes from tasting of honey, fresh-cut grass, and flowers to tasting like a mellow gingery wine. Left for several years, it makes a treasured gift for your closest wine-drinking friends.

Old Crabby Mead makes a splendid companion to cheese and crackers or any dessert. It is almost like sherry: intense and complex, with just enough sweetness to keep you coming back for more. For a summertime treat, cut this mead with club soda and add a bit of fruit juice. Old Crabby Mead develops a great fizziness if you add priming sugar before bottling.

1. Warm the honey by placing the jar in a bowl of hot water.

2. Heat the fruit juice to lukewarm (approximately 100–105°F), and sprinkle with the yeast. Set the mixture aside to let it proof.

3. Heat the juice in a large pot, add the ginger, and simmer, uncovered, 5–10 minutes. The longer the ginger cooks, the more pronounced the flavor.

4. Pour the warm honey into a sterilized 1-gallon fermentation jug.

5. Strain the juice and ginger mixture into the jug. Swirl vigorously to mix honey and juice.

6. Add the raisins and fill the jug the rest of the way with the filtered water, leaving enough room to add the yeast mixture.

Cook's Tip

Try substituting chopped rhubarb stalks for the crab apples and calling this "Old Rhuby Mead" instead!

7. Allow the mixture to cool; when it is lukewarm (100–105°F), add the proofed yeast mixture.

8. Stopper the jug with a sterilized airlock, and check in 1 hour to make sure the airlock is bubbling.

9. Set the jug in a cool, dark place until the bubbling stops and the liquid clears. This fermentation can take 2 weeks to several months. Don't be concerned about how the mixture looks after a few weeks, as it may darken during fermentation. If the bubbling stops unexpectedly, see the Troubleshooting Guide for Fermentation (page 128).

10. Rack the mead. (This may be repeated several times until mead has cleared.)

11. Bottle the mead, and let it age for at least 6 months. The mead improves after 1 year or more.

Optional: **MAKE IT SPARKLE!**

- To create an effervescent mead, rack the mead into a clean jug.

- Dissolve 2 heaping tablespoons of priming sugar in a small amount of warm water, and add to the jug.

- Swirl the mead to distribute the dissolved sugar and bottle immediately.

OLD CRABBY MEAD

spiced apple mead

INGREDIENTS

- 1 quart honey by volume (about 3 pounds)
- 1 cup Crab Apple Juice (page 80)
- 2 teaspoons (1 packet) Pasteur Champagne yeast or yeast for white wine
- 2 quarts Apple Juice (page 83)
- 1 inch fresh ginger, grated
- 2 tablespoons commercial mulling spice or homemade spice mix (see Cook's Tip)
- ½ cup raisins (not golden)
- 2 quarts filtered water
- 2 heaping tablespoons priming sugar (optional)

PULL A CHAIR UP to the fireplace, wrap yourself in a warm shawl, and open a bottle of Spiced Apple Mead. Or take a bottle or two on a big fall picnic and hike. It's that kind of autumnal drink, golden and full of interesting flavors.

Instead of using a ready-made mulling spice, you can mix your own from ingredients such as cinnamon sticks, peppercorns, cloves, cardamom pods, lemon peel, and allspice berries. Mix up a cup or so of dried herbs and use a little bit as needed. Keep the mixture in a tightly closed jar.

Experiment with adding a bit of crystallized ginger to the fresh ginger. The addition of spice tea to the brew after the first racking gives this mead an almost gingerbread aroma. Very homey!

We used Crab Apple Juice in the recipe for proofing the yeast to intensify the apple flavor. If you don't have any on hand, any juice will work for proofing the yeast.

Makes approximately 1 gallon

PREP TIME: About 1 hour, plus time for fermenting and bottling

1. **Warm the honey** by placing the jar in a bowl of hot water.

2. **Heat the Crab Apple Juice** to lukewarm (approximately 100–105°F), and sprinkle with the yeast. Set the mixture aside to let it proof.

3. **Heat the Apple Juice,** the ginger, and the mulling spice, and simmer, uncovered, 5–10 minutes. The longer the ginger and mulling spice cooks, the more pronounced the flavor.

4. **Pour the honey** into a sterilized 1-gallon fermentation jug.

5. **Strain the juice-ginger-spice** mixture, and pour into the jug. Swirl vigorously to mix honey and juice.

6. **Add the raisins** and fill the jug the rest of the way with filtered water, leaving enough room to add the yeast mixture.

7. **Allow the mixture** to cool; when it is lukewarm (100–105°F), add the proofed yeast mixture.

8. **Stopper the jug** with a sterilized airlock, and check in 1 hour to make sure the airlock is bubbling.

9. **Set the jug** in a cool, dark place until the bubbling stops and the liquid clears. This fermentation can take 2 weeks to several months. Don't be concerned about how the mixture looks after a few weeks, as it may darken during fermentation. If the bubbling stops unexpectedly, see the Troubleshooting Guide for Fermentation (page 128).

10. **Rack the mead.** (This may be repeated several times until mead has cleared.)

11. **Bottle the mead,** and let it age for at least 6 months. The mead improves after 1 year or more.

Optional: **MAKE IT SPARKLE!**
- To create an effervescent mead, rack the mead into a clean jug.

- Dissolve 2 heaping tablespoons of priming sugar in a small amount of warm water, and add to the jug.

- Swirl the mead to distribute the dissolved sugar and bottle immediately.

Cook's Tip

Taste the mead after the first rack. If the spices are too subtle, make a strong tea of additional mulling spice and add it to the fermentation jug during the racking process. When we first made this recipe, it wasn't spicy enough. So before bottling we made a tea of 3 cinnamon sticks, 10 black peppercorns, 10 cardamom pods, and 10 allspice berries, and added it to the mix. The result was extra spicy and super delicious.

very perry holiday mead

HERE'S ONE MORE REASON to harvest and process pears, no matter where you find them. (We get our pears from a favorite tree on a vacant lot.) We love this mead. It's spicy and has plenty of pear flavor, and the longer it sits in the bottle the better it gets.

Very Perry Holiday Mead is a seasonal sensation to serve in small glasses when friends drop by at the holidays. The color is mellow gold and crystal clear, like a wonderful ornament on the table. If you can bear to part with any, it makes a lovely gift in decorative bottles.

Makes approximately 1 gallon

PREP TIME: About 1 hour, plus time for fermenting and bottling

INGREDIENTS

- 2 quarts filtered water
- 1 quart honey by volume (about 3 pounds)
- 1 cup any fruit juice
- 2 teaspoons (1 packet) Pasteur Champagne yeast or yeast for white wine
- 2 quarts Peerless Pear Cider (page 86)
- ½ cup raisins (not golden)
- ½ cinnamon stick
- 5 cardamom pods
- 3 whole cloves
- 2 heaping tablespoons priming sugar (optional)

   Additional pear cider to add during racking (optional)

1. Bring the water to a boil in a kettle.

2. Warm the honey by placing the jar in a bowl of hot water.

3. Heat the fruit juice to lukewarm (approximately 100–105°F), and sprinkle with the yeast. Set the mixture aside to let it proof.

4. Pour the warm honey into a sterilized 1-gallon fermentation jug.

5. Pour 2 cups of the boiling water into the jug, and swirl or shake it until honey is dissolved.

6. Add the Peerless Pear Cider, and swirl vigorously to mix.

7. Add the raisins and spices and fill the jug the rest of the way with filtered water, leaving enough room to add the yeast mixture.

8. Allow the mixture to cool; when it is lukewarm (100–105°F), add the proofed yeast mixture.

9. Stopper the jug with a sterilized airlock, and check in 1 hour to make sure the airlock is bubbling.

10. Set the jug in a cool, dark place until the bubbling stops and the liquid clears. This fermentation can take 2 weeks to several months. Don't be concerned about how the mixture looks after a few weeks, as it may darken during fermentation. If the bubbling stops unexpectedly, see the Troubleshooting Guide for Fermentation (page 128).

11. Rack the mead. (This may be repeated several times until mead has cleared.)

12. Bottle the mead, and let it age for at least 6 months. The mead improves after 1 year or more.

Optional: **MAKE IT SPARKLE!**

- To create an effervescent mead, rack the mead into a clean jug.

- Dissolve 2 heaping tablespoons of priming sugar in a small amount of warm water, and add to the jug.

- Swirl the mead to distribute the dissolved sugar and bottle immediately.

Cook's Tip

For extra flavor, freeze a cup or more extra Peerless Pear Cider, to thaw and add to the mead during the racking phase.

crab apple rice wine

INGREDIENTS

- 2 quarts filtered water
- 1 quart Crab Apple Juice (page 80)
- 2 teaspoons (1 packet) Champagne yeast or yeast for white wine
- 4½ cups uncooked rice, any kind
- 3 cups sugar
- ½ cup raisins (not golden)

THIS IS UNLIKE ANY SAKE you've ever tasted. We made up this recipe to take advantage of the usual huge crab apple harvest that comes in late summer. Rice wine makes an interesting base for experimentation, as the first sip tastes of fruit but then dissolves into a gentle rice glow.

Don't confuse this beverage with traditional sake you buy from a grocery store or wine merchant. Regular sake uses fermentation of rice starch (as in beer) rather than of fruit sugars, plus the addition of a special koji mold to ignite the high-alcohol fermentation. Here, we make a rice wine from the fermentation of rice plus regular Champagne or white wine yeast. This recipe uses fruit, too, and thus is not true sake. The color is golden rather than clear.

No matter. This drink is luscious hot or cold, and makes a spirited companion for a sushi dinner at home.

Note that rice wine proportions needn't be precise and that rice wine does not need to age long in the bottle; drink it young.

Makes approximately 1 gallon

PREP TIME: About a ½ hour, plus time for fermenting and bottling

1. Bring the water to a boil.

2. Heat 1 cup of juice to lukewarm (approximately 100–105°F), and sprinkle with the yeast. Set the mixture aside to let it proof.

3. Put the rice, sugar, and raisins in the jug, then pour in the boiling water. Shake the jug vigorously to mix the contents.

4. Add the remaining juice to the jug, filling it to the shoulders, leaving enough room to add the yeast mixture..

5. Allow the mixture to cool; when it is lukewarm (100–105°F), add the proofed yeast mixture.

6. Stopper the jug with a sterilized airlock, and check in 1 hour to make sure the airlock is bubbling.

7. Set the jug in a cool, dark place until the bubbling stops and the liquid clears.

8. During the first week of fermentation, gently swirl the jug to distribute the yeast throughout the rice sediment. Fermentation can take 2 to 3 weeks.

9. Rack the wine. (This may be repeated several times until wine has cleared.)

10. Bottle the wine. This beverage can be ready as early as 1 month after the brew date.

start with
crab apple juice

Cook's Tip

This rice wine can be used as an inexpensive alternative for any recipe calling for sake, with outstanding results. The next time you sauté kale or other green leafy vegetables, mix about a tablespoon of miso (fermented soybean paste) with 2 or 3 tablespoons of Crab Apple Rice Wine, and toss with the cooked greens for a delicious Asian twist to an old garden favorite.

CRAB APPLE RICE WINE

nan's crab apple supercider

We hit a home run out of the park the first time we tried this recipe: The result was fresh, aromatic, and bursting with flavor. We racked the cider once at three weeks of fermentation, topping it up with a bit of apple juice and some pear cider, and adding a few more grape skins. We racked it again a week later and it was perfect, both to drink and as a digestive.

Makes approximately 1 gallon

PREP TIME: About ½ hour, plus time for fermenting and bottling

UNLIKE TYPICAL APPLE CIDER, which comes off the fruit press cloudy and thick, Nan's Crab Apple SuperCider is crystal-clear from the start. You've never tasted anything like it. This beverage can be quite tart compared to apple cider, thanks to its high tannin and acid content, but certain crab apple varieties carry a load of sugar and can make for a sublime taste.

Be sure to start with the crab apple cider (see Apple Family Cider, page 85) at room temperature rather than chilled so that the wild yeast action gets a fast start. A large differential between yeast and liquid temperatures can shock the yeast into inactivity.

This recipe is unusual in having no added wine yeast. Instead, fermentation comes from raisins and from wild yeast present on the apple skins.

NOTE: Wild yeast varies considerably from location to location, and using it can be risky in fermentation. If a rogue yeast or bacterium overwhelms the regular fermentation process, the batch will fail. However, if all goes well, the results are exciting.

INGREDIENTS

- 1 gallon freshly pressed, unpasteurized crab apple cider at room temperature
- 1 cup sugar
- ½ cup raisins (not golden) or 1 cup grape skins (reserved from pressing grape cider)

1. Heat 1 cup of the crab apple cider in a small saucepan.

2. Add the sugar and stir until dissolved.

3. Pour the mixture into a sterilized 1-gallon fermentation jug.

4. Add the raisins or grape skins, and the remaining crab apple cider to fill the jug to the neck, leaving 1–2 inches of headroom. Due to the variability of wild yeast, try to minimize the headspace.

5. Stopper the jug with an airlock, and check in 1 day to make sure the airlock is bubbling. If there is no evidence of yeast action (bubbling) after a day, activate a packet of dry wine or cider yeast and pitch it into the jug.

6. Set the jug in a cool, dark place for several weeks, until active fermentation slows. Don't be concerned about how the mixture looks, as it may change color during fermentation. If the bubbling stops unexpectedly, see the Troubleshooting Guide for Fermentation (page 128).

7. Rack the cider. Then rack it again in a week or so.

8. Drink the cider right away or bottle it. Beer bottles with crimped caps work well for cider.

Cook's Tip

If you're short on crab apples, use any pure garden cider (apple, grape, pear, or quince) or any late berries that you have pressed. The idea is to harness natural sugars together with wild yeast. Any combination is worth trying.

peerless perry

PERRY IS SIMPLY fermented pear cider. The beverage, similar to hard apple cider, has a long history in the Old World, as pears grew widely in parts of the British Isles, France, and the Low Countries. Though the fortunes of perry have waxed and waned as technology and agricultural methods have evolved, we think it's time to drink more perry. Why let pears rot on the ground when you can turn them into a wonderful beverage so easily and economically?

Starting with freshly pressed Peerless Pear Cider (page 86), you need add little else besides wine yeast or ale yeast: just a bit of sugar and some raisins or grape skins. Pear juice that has been heat extracted and canned will not have the natural wild yeasts needed.

Just as with hard ciders, which rely on existing yeast in the fruit skins instead of a controlled dose of agreeable wine yeast, perry may not be a uniform product from batch to batch if you choose not to add a start of standardized yeast. In fact, we have found that perry can suddenly go bad in the midst of fermentation without the extra yeast; that's a tough lesson.

Be sure to have the pear cider at room temperature rather than chilled so that the yeast action gets a fast start. A large differential between yeast and liquid temperatures can shock the yeast into inactivity.

Makes approximately 1 gallon

PREP TIME: About a ½ hour, plus overnight, plus time for fermenting and bottling

INGREDIENTS

1 **gallon freshly pressed, unpasteurized pear cider at room temperature**

2 **teaspoons (1 packet) wine yeast or ale yeast**

1 **cup sugar**

½ **cup raisins (not golden) or 1 cup grape skins reserved from pressing grape juice**

1. Heat 1 cup of the pear cider to lukewarm. Sprinkle with the yeast. Put the mixture aside to let it proof.

2. Heat an additional 1 cup of the cider in a small saucepan.

3. Add the sugar and stir until dissolved.

4. Pour the mixture into a sterilized 1-gallon fermentation jug (a large funnel makes this easier).

5. Pour the raisins or grape skins and the remaining pear cider to fill the jug to the neck, leaving enough room to add the yeast mixture. Allow the mixture to cool; when it is lukewarm (100–105°F), add the proofed yeast mixture.

6. Stopper the jug with an airlock, and check in 1 hour to make sure the airlock is bubbling.

7. Set the jug in a cool, dark place for several weeks, until active fermentation slows. Don't be concerned about how the mixture looks, as it may change color during fermentation. If the bubbling stops unexpectedly, see the Troubleshooting Guide for Fermentation (page 128).

8. Rack the cider. Then rack it again in a week or so.

9. Drink the cider right away or bottle it. Beer bottles with crimped caps work well for cider.

Cook's Tip

For a spiced variation, drop one or two cinnamon sticks into the fermentation jug when you assemble the perry.

luscious limoncello

INGREDIENTS

- 8 organic homegrown lemons
- 1 quart vodka
- 1 quart filtered water
- 3¾ cups sugar

LIMONCELLO (pronounced "lee-mun-*chell*-o"), or lemon liqueur, may not be to everyone's taste, but if you have organic lemons on hand, we say, "Flaunt it, baby, flaunt it!"

This is a folk recipe, hailing from southern Italian regions, so feel free to experiment wildly according to your own taste. In fact, why stick to lemons? You may be able to use another citrus fruit, or a mixture of fruits, to make equally refreshing, exciting after-dinner drinks: tangerine, kumquat, blood orange, or even sweet lime.

Two things to keep in mind when making limoncello: First, grate only the outer, colored peel of the citrus to use, leaving the bitter white pith behind. Second, build in plenty of time for the citrus peel to steep in alcohol. Existing recipes call for anywhere from 40 to 80 days in that step alone, with another month of aging after further assembly. The result is a very sweet, rich, yet naturally astringent liqueur to sip in tiny glasses after dinner.

This recipe can easily be halved or doubled. The more you make, though, the more you can package in decorative stoppered bottles to give as gifts.

Makes 2 quarts

PREP TIME: 1 to 2 hours, plus several months to steep

1. Rinse the lemons, then grate the outer zest using a fine zester, being careful not to use any of the white inner pith. Grating over a sheet of parchment paper makes collecting and handling the zest easier. The zest should be about the consistency of grated Parmesan cheese. Use the rest of the lemons for other dishes.

2. Empty the grated lemon zest into a clean half-gallon jar with a tight-fitting lid, then add the vodka. Close the jar and store it in a cool closet or pantry for 1 to 3 months, or longer. Use two quart-size jars if necessary.

3. After the mixture has steeped, boil the water in a saucepan, add the sugar, and cook for 5 minutes, until the sugar has dissolved. Remove from the heat, and let the mixture cool to room temperature.

4. Add the sugar syrup to the jar, cover the jar, and return it to a cool place to steep another month or more.

5. When this step is finished, strain the liquid through several layers of cheesecloth moistened with filtered water, or it may be necessary to run the liquid through several paper coffee filters. Pour the limoncello into smaller bottles using a funnel, and seal with stoppers.

Keep the finished limoncello in the freezer, and serve it very cold. If you prefer to drink a lighter beverage, use the liqueur with mixers such as club soda, lemonade, or sparkling wine.

part 3
syrups & teas

6

creating garden syrups

Mary Poppins was right! A spoonful of sugar *does* help the medicine go down.

No matter what ails you in life (quick — think of something), you're likely to feel better with a stout mug of some warm, aromatic beverage cradled in your hands or with a fizzy, fruity summer drink within reach. Not to mention delicious waves of flavor rolling down a stack of steaming griddle cakes or a slow avalanche of liquid mint sliding down a mountain of chocolate ice cream.

See what we mean? Life without sugar is strictly to be avoided. A little sugar is fine for most of us once in a while, and syrups consist of nothing but sweetener and flavorings. Adding sugar to fruit juice intensifies the delicate fruit flavor and adds to the versatility of your harvest.

There's no — repeat *no* — reason to run to the grocery store anymore for syrups and beverage mixers. And there's no need to pay big bucks for gourmet syrups in fancy shops. You grow the ingredients, you put them together. Bottle them up in pretty swing-top bottles, and you'll always have a unique hostess gift ready to take to the next party.

the beauty of homemade syrups

WE LOVE MAKING GARDEN SYRUPS for many reasons. In previous chapters we devoted considerable space to admittedly time-consuming methods of preserving large quantities of high-yield crops. Syrups, in contrast, are all about small and fast.

For example, you don't have to process syrups in a boiling-water bath, since they have a fairly long natural shelf life even if you don't refrigerate them. Skipping the water bath saves water, too, of course. When all you need is a spoonful, small and fast means:

- Using just two cups of juice, or a quart at most, to make several small bottles of syrup.

- Not having to wait — syrup-making process often takes just 15 to 20 minutes.

- Capturing the goodness from left-over bits of fruit, herbs, or spices.

- Controlling the consistency of the finished product, from thick to thin.

- Being able to use spare minutes during a busy harvest season, rather than scheduling a whole day.

In modern cooking, syrups are primarily used as mixers with other beverages. Thus, peach or berry syrup can be a pleasant addition to anything from club soda to coffee to herbal tea. Add a little fruit syrup to yogurt, to a breakfast smoothie, or to a milkshake. Fruit syrups in particular can also be used as delicious coloring agents in cream frostings. A dash of fruit syrup goes nicely over pastries, ice cream, or pie.

Use it to augment the milk on top of dried cereal or granola, or to add pizzazz to cooked cereals like oatmeal or creamed wheat. And of course, fruit syrups can act as distinctive sweeteners in such recipes as salad dressings, sauces, and marinades, or to flavor a batch of home-brewed beer. In a pinch, you can use a full-bodied fruit or fruit-herb syrup to sweeten homemade salad dressing that has too much vinegar.

FOR PROOFING YEAST

Use homemade syrups in place of fruit juice to activate (proof) yeast, whether in breadmaking or winemaking. Simply dilute several tablespoons of the syrup in a cup of lukewarm water.

Homemade syrups are quick and easy, and they store well in swing-top bottles for up to a year, with ascorbic acid added, or six months without it. They have a long shelf life because they're boiled, which kills bacteria, yeast, and mold. In addition, the sugar itself has preservative properties, as well as helping keep a syrup's color and flavor bright.

We've developed an intriguing range of spiced syrups and syrups flavored with such robust herbs as rosemary and bay leaf. We offer a few herbal ideas merely as an introduction to the endless possibilities in nature's wonderland of herbs and flowers. By the way, any of these recipes can be made with store-bought juice instead of homemade. Just be sure to use organic juice with no additives. One advantage of using store-bought juice is that the solids already have been processed out so there's no foam to skim and the result is a perfectly clear product.

PERFUMED DESERT WINDS

We love making garden syrups for the romance. For what is syrup? The Arabic and Latin languages have similar words that simply mean beverage, or fruit boiled with sugar. *Sharab* comes from the Arabic verb "to drink," and the later Latin word *siropus* is derived circuitously from the same origin; the old English drink called a shrub also grew from those roots. It does not matter which sweetener is used (cane sugar, white sugar, palm sugar, molasses, or something else entirely), although characteristics of the finished products will vary greatly. Molasses or honey will quickly overpower the flavor of the syrup if you are not careful.

For us, the romance of syrup is mingled with the allure of rarity: a rose blooming in a desert oasis, saffron threads and cardamom pods carried from afar, a melon watered by hand, mint growing near a spring, bay leaves teased into plump glossy spears. All syrups made from such ingredients include a secret ingredient: mystery. Can't you just taste it on the tip of your tongue?

Desert dwellers of ancient Persia may hold the edge in syrup romance, but other cultures around the world doubtless think of their own syrups as equally authentic, and we celebrate them all.

just add sugar and boil!

OUR SYRUP RECIPES don't call for anything special in the way of equipment. Just make sure your pots and pans, utensils, and other pieces of equipment are all nonreactive, that is, stainless steel, glass, or enamel. No copper or aluminum anything, or the result will be a discolored and unappealing syrup.

The principle of tasty syrup is to boil a flavoring, often juice, with sugar until the ingredients are blended. Period. Of course, there are exceptions. In the case of very concentrated syrup, like watermelon, the idea is actually to boil down the thin, sweet juice until it becomes thick. Even that doesn't take terribly long.

And in some recipes using herbs, flowers, or spices for the main flavoring, the method is to make a "tea" by steeping the ingredients for the specified time and then boiling that tea with sugar. Alternatively, some syrups get their spice ingredients at the end, after the boiling. That way the spices don't give the syrup a burned or bitter taste.

The time of year for producing homegrown syrups, for us anyway, begins in late spring or early summer with seasonal harvests of herbs, berries, and succulent orchard fruits like peaches and cherries. Whenever you make and can juices at that time of year, even if you don't process syrups right then, you have already done the bulk of syrup preparation work.

There's a break in the action during midsummer. Then, as late summer and early autumn crops come in (apples, quince, watermelon, prickly pear cactus), there is another round of syrup making.

cleaning, labeling, and storage

Of course you need clean little bottles for syrups, but the sanitation requirements are not as cumbersome as with canning or fermentation. Running the bottles through the dishwasher or a sinkful of hot suds followed by a swirl of boiling water is enough to sterilize them. Same thing with your little funnel.

Swing-top bottles have a cool, old-timey look; the ones we favor have a porcelain cap attached loosely with a metal collar. The inner edge of the cap has a rubbery surface with a little give. To close the bottle, swing the cap upright and snap down one arm of the metal collar. The bottles come in various sizes; we suggest starting small, say eight ounces, and there may not be any reason to go bigger. These reusable bottles are widely available at kitchen supply stores and online. The gaskets eventually become brittle, but many retailers carry replacements.

If you are processing large batches of syrups, it's fine to use mason jars. In that case do go ahead and seal the filled jars of syrup in a boiling-water bath to prolong shelf life. Otherwise, with swing-top bottles just pour the hot syrup into the bottles using a funnel; hot equipment makes for better seals.

As with any other homemade product, label your bottles promptly once they have cooled. Your label should list the name of the item, the ingredients if you wish, and the date bottled.

If you have added ascorbic acid during cooking, shelf life is about a year in a cool, dark cupboard. Without ascorbic acid, don't keep bottles in the cupboard longer than six months. Once opened, the bottles should be refrigerated.

Discard any syrup that has fuzz on top or otherwise looks not quite right.

And now, isn't it time for a cool, refreshing drink made with an interesting homegrown syrup?

IT'S ALL IN THE RATIO

The ratio of sugar or other sweetener to fruit juice determines the thickness of the syrup. Our basic recipe (page 182) uses a 1:1 ratio of sugar to fruit juice, which creates a heavy syrup. For lighter syrup, reduce the sugar ratio by up to half, or 1 part sugar to 2 parts juice. To make a super-sweet, extra-heavy syrup, double the proportion of sugar (2 parts sugar to 1 part juice).

In the case of pomegranate juice, this thicker syrup is sometimes called Poor Man's Grenadine and makes a nice addition to many cocktails.

Keep in mind that the lower the sugar ratio, the shorter is the shelf life of any syrup. The more sugar, the longer the syrup will last on the shelf. Weird, no?

how to make syrup

1. Combine the ingredients in a nonreactive saucepan or pot and bring to a boil, stirring to dissolve the sugar. Here we're making Blueberry-Basil Syrup (page 188).

2. Remove from heat or simmer as called for in recipe. To make filling the bottles easier, lift the bulk of the herbs from the pot with a skimmer or "spider." Skim off any foam that remains.

3. Use a glass measuring cup or ladle to pour the syrup through a screened funnel to remove any stray sediment into clean swing-top bottles or other glass containers.

4. Water-bath processing isn't necessary with syrups; just sterilize bottles or jars before filling them. Don't forget the labels!

BLUEBERRY-BASIL SYRUP
IN CLUB SODA

garden syrups

fruit juice syrup

HERE IS OUR not-at-all-complicated method for making delicious fruit syrup:

STEP 1: Make one of the fruit juices from chapter 4, and can it.

STEP 2: When the spirit moves you, take out a jar, add sugar, boil, and bottle.

You can make this basic recipe with any prepared juice, such as berry, strawberry, peach, grape, or cherry. We tested all kinds of variables: different fruits, a variety of sweeteners, dried and fresh herbs.

As noted on page 177, the thickness of the syrup depends on the ratio of sugar or other sweetener to fruit juice. Here we use a 1-to-1 ratio of sugar to fruit juice to make a heavy syrup. To make the syrup lighter, reduce the sugar by up to half; to make it even heavier, double the proportion of sugar.

Makes 1 pint

PREP TIME: 10 minutes, using prepared fruit juice

INGREDIENTS

- 2 cups fruit juice
- 2 cups sugar
- ⅛ teaspoon ascorbic acid (omit if prepared juice already has ascorbic acid added)

1. Combine the juice and sugar in a saucepan, and bring to a full boil, stirring occasionally to dissolve the sugar. Skim off any foam that may have formed.

2. Remove from the heat.

3. Add the ascorbic acid if needed, and stir.

4. Pour the contents into sterilized containers, seal, and label.

This syrup can be used immediately or stored in swing-top bottles for up to a year with ascorbic acid added, or six months without it. Store in the refrigerator for up to two weeks after opening.

SWEETS FOR THE SWEET

Be careful using natural sweeteners such as molasses or raw cane sugar. The flavor can be very strong, and these sweeteners may create a lot of foam as they cook.

Use white sugar for crystal-clear syrup; other sugars may produce a darker product, anything from the palest spun gold to dark honey amber.

Experiment, and use any combination of sweeteners you like.

mint syrup

INGREDIENTS

2 cups filtered water

1 cup mint leaves, washed

2 cups sugar

⅛ teaspoon ascorbic acid

THE TASTE OF MINT has never been so perfectly fresh and sweet as in this syrup. Garden mint really sings when boiled with sugar, and whatever this syrup is added to will be energized with minty goodness.

Here are just some of the beverages you can make using mint syrup: mojitos, mint juleps, mint-flavored iced tea or lemonade, mint spritzers, minty-licious sangria or other wine punch, or mint-flavored hot chocolate (with a splash of peppermint schnapps for the adult version). For a special dessert, add some mint syrup to homemade fudge sauce before spooning it over ice cream.

Makes 1 pint

PREP TIME: 1 hour

1. **Bring the water** to a boil.

2. **Place the mint** leaves in a small bowl, and pour the boiling water over them. Cover and steep for 20 minutes.

3. **Strain the liquid** into a saucepan to remove the mint leaves.

4. **Add the sugar** and bring to a boil. Skim off any foam.

5. **Remove from the** heat.

6. **Add the ascorbic** acid and stir.

7. **Pour the contents** into sterilized containers, seal, and label.

This syrup can be used immediately or stored in swing-top bottles for up to a year with ascorbic acid added, or six months without it. Store in the refrigerator for up to two weeks after opening.

Cook's Tip

Instead of mint, try other herbs for a savory experience: basil, lemon balm, bee balm, lavender, orange blossom, or rose hip. Herb syrups taste even more special with a little added honey, a few drops of corn syrup, or both. (Shh! Don't tell.)

water-melon-mint syrup

WHAT A GREAT TASTE combo! The result is unique and worthwhile, for the watermelon takes some of the sugary sweetness out of all-mint syrup and adds a shade of vegetable-patch summer flavor.

It's important to skim the foam off the top of this syrup for the clearest product possible.

Makes 2 pints

PREP TIME: 1–2 hours

INGREDIENTS

1 whole small watermelon or a ½ large watermelon (approximately 8 cups of fruit, enough to produce 4 cups of strained liquid), with rind removed and cut into chunks

½ cup mint leaves, stripped of stems

4 cups sugar

¼ teaspoon ascorbic acid

1. Place the watermelon chunks, including seeds, into a food processor. Using the "pulse" setting, process until juice forms, just a few seconds. The seeds will sink to the bottom.

2. Strain 4 cups of the watermelon juice through 2 layers of dampened cheesecloth into a saucepan, and bring to a boil. Skim off any foam.

3. Remove from the heat.

4. Add the mint leaves. Cover and let steep for 20 minutes.

5. Strain the mixture again into a clean saucepan. Add the sugar and bring to a boil. Skim off any foam.

6. Add the ascorbic acid and stir.

7. Strain the contents yet again into sterilized containers, seal, and label. Watermelon pulp is hard to remove completely, so the extra straining is required for clearer syrup.

This syrup can be used immediately or stored in swing-top bottles for up to a year with ascorbic acid added, or six months without it. Store in the refrigerator for up to two weeks after opening.

Cook's Tip

It's not necessary to use seedless watermelons. If you use the pulse setting on your food processor to liquefy the pulp, the seeds will settle to the bottom and can be easily strained out.

Yogurt and
watermelon
chunks
drizzled with
watermelon-
mint syrup

concen-trated watermelon syrup

INGREDIENTS

2 whole small watermelons or 1 large watermelon (approximately 12 cups of fruit, enough to produce 8 cups of strained liquid), rind removed and cut into chunks

Filtered water

Ascorbic acid, ⅛ teaspoon per pint of syrup

WATERMELONS GROW ABUNDANTLY, and there comes a time in late summer when grocery stores, farmers' markets, and even home gardens overflow with this delicious and highly nutritious fruit. Is there a way to preserve this fleeting bounty? Yes!

The finished syrup has an interesting, almost savory, flavor and a thick, granular texture; it's not just sweet but carries a bit of the earth with it, like the gourd that watermelon is. Try it in coffee or add it to breakfast yogurt. If you're a brewer, experiment with this concentrate to flavor some home-brewed pumpkin ale.

This syrup generates a lot of foam as it boils, since watermelon is naturally high in sugar (as well as in vitamins A and C, and minerals). We recommend a double straining process for a clearer product: straining the pulp before cooking it down, then letting it settle overnight.

Makes 1 pint

PREP TIME: 1–2 hours, plus overnight for solids to settle

1. Line a large colander with two layers of cheesecloth dampened with filtered water. Set the colander over a 2-quart bowl or measuring container.

2. Process the fruit in a food processor to release the juice.

3. Pour the processed fruit into the colander to strain out the pulp. Let the resulting juice sit overnight in a refrigerator for solids to settle.

4. The next day carefully ladle the juice off the sediments.

5. Pour the strained juice into a large nonreactive stockpot, and bring to a boil. Continue boiling until the liquid is reduced by three-quarters.

6. Add the ascorbic acid and stir.

7. Pour the contents into sterilized containers, seal, and label. Store in the refrigerator for up to 6 months.

peach-rosemary syrup

INGREDIENTS

- 2 cups Peach Juice (page 76)
- 2 cups sugar
- 2 sprigs rosemary (5–6 inches), rinsed
- ⅛ teaspoon ascorbic acid (omit if prepared juice already has ascorbic acid added)

1. Combine the juice, sugar, and rosemary sprigs in a saucepan, and bring to a boil. Skim off any foam.

2. Remove from the heat.

3. Add ascorbic acid if needed and stir.

4. Remove the rosemary.

5. Pour into sterilized containers, seal, and label.

This syrup can be used immediately or stored in swing-top bottles for up to a year with ascorbic acid added, or six months without it. Store in the refrigerator for up to two weeks after opening.

THIS SYRUP reaches new culinary heights with the addition of some fresh rosemary that may be crowding your garden. The dynamic flavor combination is timeless, like a medieval feast brought to life.

Peach juice, to be honest, has a low flavor profile that improves with a variety of partners in syrup form, anything from herbs like rosemary or basil, to spices like cardamom or star anise or peppercorns, to accents like citrus or ginger. Different combinations can create a veritable symphony of flavor notes.

Our recipe suggestion with this syrup is the Peach-Rosemary Fizz Cocktail: 1 part silver rum and 1 part Peach-Rosemary Syrup, served over ice with a splash of club soda and a lime slice for garnish.

Makes 1 pint

PREP TIME: 10 minutes

Cook's Tip

This recipe, like other syrups, is easily doubled or tripled, but herbs could be overpowering in those quantities. If using strong herbs such as peppercorns, bay leaves, or rosemary, do not add too much when increasing the juice and sugar proportions. Just bump up the herb amounts slightly.

blueberry-basil syrup

INGREDIENTS

- 2 cups blueberry juice
- 2 cups raw cane sugar
- 1 cup fresh basil leaves
- ⅛ teaspoon ascorbic acid (omit if prepared juice already has ascorbic acid added)

1. Combine the juice, sugar, and basil leaves in a saucepan, and bring to a full boil. Reduce the heat, and simmer 5 minutes. Skim off any foam.

2. Remove from the heat.

3. Add ascorbic acid if needed and stir.

4. Strain out the basil leaves. Pour into sterilized containers, seal, and label.

This syrup can be used immediately or stored in swing-top bottles for up to a year with ascorbic acid added, or six months without it. Store in the refrigerator for up to two weeks after opening.

USE THIS UNUSUAL SYRUP for almost anything at all; it has a sophisticated and unexpected flavor that preserves the complexity of basil with the heavy fruitiness of blueberry. Raw cane sugar, rather than white sugar, imparts even more flavor notes, creating a dark, velvety liquid.

You can make blueberry juice following the recipe for Berry Juice (page 72). Try to avoid splattering as you cook, because blueberries will stain.

A spectacular variation on this syrup is to substitute 6 fresh bay leaves (or 4 dried) for the basil. The result is subtly spicy and makes a wonderful addition to cocktails or any recipe calling for a glaze.

Makes 1 pint

PREP TIME: 10 minutes, if using prepared fruit juice

Cook's Tip

If the syrup is allowed to boil too long it will thicken into jelly and not pour from a bottle. This happy accident happened to us, but the resulting jelly was delicious. It's perfect on toast, or served with sliced meats and cheese, adding a bit of savory sweetness to any appetizer.

spiced ginger-bay syrup

INGREDIENTS

2 cups water

2 cups sugar

6 fresh bay leaves or 4 dried, crushed

2 inches fresh ginger, coarsely chopped

⅛ teaspoon ascorbic acid

10 saffron threads, 8 peppercorns, 4 cardamom pods, 4 whole cloves, 2 cinnamon sticks, singly or in any combination (optional)

A BAY LAUREL TREE is surprisingly easy to grow and adds tremendously to home cooking once established. Gardeners in mild climates can treat the bay tree as an evergreen, planting it as a hedge or singly as a specimen tree or topiary, but in colder climates the bay must be wrapped to protect it against winter's ice and winds, or swaddled in mulch; even so, it may well lose some of its leaves. You can also grow bay in a pot that can come indoors.

No matter how the tree grows, the dark green glossy leaves have a unique aroma that seems to bind together disparate flavors. Though bay leaves are usually used in soups and stews, here they flavor this mild syrup, which makes an interesting drink base for cocktails or a wonderful surprise for saturating pound cake.

Makes 1 pint

PREP TIME: 10 minutes

1. Combine the water, sugar, bay leaves, and ginger in a saucepan and bring to a full boil, stirring occasionally to dissolve the sugar. Lower the heat and simmer for 5 minutes.

2. Remove from the heat.

3. Add the ascorbic acid and stir.

4. Divide whatever whole spices you are using equally between the sterilized containers.

5. Strain the syrup to remove ginger and bay leaves. Pour into the containers, seal, and label. Except for saffron, the spices may float to the top.

This syrup can be used immediately or stored in swing-top bottles for up to a year with ascorbic acid added, or six months without it. Store in the refrigerator for up to two weeks after opening.

Cook's Tip

Feel free to experiment with ginger-bay syrup by adding other spices. We tested these combinations and loved them: cinnamon with cardamom pods and whole cloves, black peppercorns and cardamom pods, and saffron threads alone. Because saffron is so pricey, we only used a small amount for this one recipe. But the flavor and color are so pleasing that it's worth a mention. Do not grind the spices; put them whole into the bottles and pour the syrup on top of them.

one world apple spice syrup

INGREDIENTS

2 cups Apple Juice (page 83)

¾ cup sugar

¼ cup blackstrap molasses

Juice and rind of 1 lemon

¼ teaspoon ground nutmeg

4 cardamom pods

1 cinnamon stick

⅛ teaspoon ascorbic acid (omit if prepared juice already has ascorbic acid added)

IF YOU WANT TO SHAKE UP a recipe that ordinarily calls for soy sauce, try adding a little of this yummy syrup as well. We originally called it Old World Apple Spice Syrup until we realized that the constituent blackstrap molasses is American.

The sugar notes, tempered with lemon and spices, can liven up modern stir-fry dishes by increasing the carmelization factor. Likewise, this syrup adds depth to such standards as beef stew, fruit compote, or roasted root crops.

Don't be tempted to add more molasses, as it can quickly overpower the apple juice and spices.

Makes 1 pint

PREP TIME: 10 minutes

1. Combine the apple juice, sugar, molasses, lemon juice and rind, and nutmeg, cardamom, and cinnamon in a saucepan and bring to a boil. Skim off any foam.

2. Remove from the heat.

3. Add ascorbic acid if needed and stir.

4. Strain out the solid ingredients and pour into sterilized containers, seal, and label.

This syrup can be used immediately or stored in swing-top bottles for up to a year with ascorbic acid added, or six months without it. Store in the refrigerator for up to two weeks after opening.

Cook's Tip

Use a half-and-half combination of One World Apple Spice Syrup and white wine to deglaze the turkey roasting pan at Thanksgiving. Your gravy will get raves!

tart
cherry
syrup

INGREDIENTS

- 2 **cups pure cherry juice**
- 1 **cup sugar**
- ⅛ **teaspoon ascorbic acid (omit if prepared juice already has ascorbic acid added)**

1. Bring the cherry juice and sugar to a boil. Skim off any foam.

2. Remove from the heat.

3. Add ascorbic acid if needed and stir.

4. Pour the contents into sterilized containers, seal, and label.

This syrup can be used immediately or stored in swing-top bottles for up to six months rather than a year, because of the lighter sugar content. Store in the refrigerator for up to two weeks after opening.

GROWING CHERRIES MAY SEEM EASY, but getting all the way to harvest can be a challenge. Birds, weather, and branches that grow too high and too fast can all frustrate the home gardener. We include this syrup because the taste of tart cherry juice is fantastic, and cherries are a top health food. If it isn't possible to make your own, you can use any pure, unsweetened cherry juice, preferably organic.

To preserve the incomparable tartness of the juice, we have turned this into a super-light recipe by using only half the usual proportion of sugar.

Makes 1 pint

PREP TIME: 10 minutes

Cook's Tip

Remember Cherry Coke? Make your own fountain drink by adding several tablespoons of tart cherry syrup to a glass of Coca-Cola or other carbonated beverage over ice.

prickly
pear
cactus
syrup

INGREDIENTS

4 cups Prickly Pear Cactus Juice (page 90)

2 cups sugar

1. Combine the juice and sugar in a saucepan, and bring to a full boil, stirring occasionally to dissolve the sugar. Skim off any foam.

2. Remove from the heat.

3. Pour the contents into sterilized containers, seal, and label.

This syrup can be used immediately or stored in swing-top bottles for up to six months rather than a year, because of the lighter sugar content. Store in the refrigerator for up to two weeks after opening.

THIS SYRUP IS USEFUL many ways: as a basting liquid for roast meat or poultry, a coloring agent for pink icing, an ingredient for party punch, a flavoring for smoothies, and much more. Because it's so healthy you can use it to tease additional nutrition into various desserts or to glazed vegetables.

Makes 1 quart

PREP TIME: 10 minutes if using already prepared juice

Cook's Tip

Peel and slice carrots lengthwise or on the bias, put into a saucepan with a bit of olive oil, plus 1–2 tablespoons of syrup, a pinch of celery seed, and enough water to come about ¾ of the way to the top of the carrots. Cover partially and cook over medium heat until water is evaporated and carrots are soft with a nice shiny glaze. Add a bit of chopped fresh parsley and serve immediately.

7 creating garden teas

Before we wax rhapsodic about the wonderful qualities of garden teas, we'd like to air a pet peeve: the mystery of why shoppers are willing to pay so much for herbal and flower teas. Imagine spending that much for something you could grow and process at home for *pennies a pound*, year after year! Based on our supermarket analysis, you may be paying over $32 a pound for teas made from nothing more than dried mint, chamomile, hibiscus, rose hips, citrus peel, catnip, licorice, or other easy-to-grow flowers and herbs. And then there's kombucha, an unusual liver tonic and all-around health drink made from a sweetened tea base.

More than a few of the special plants listed on the next page can be classified as medicinal herbs as well, and when they are marketed that way, the retail prices can go higher still. We want to help you save money by telling you how to grow the ingredients for interesting teas and then how to dry and preserve those crops yourself. When you drink teas you have plucked from the homegrown landscape, you are sipping sunshine. The flavors and the colors are *that* fresh. Once you establish these tea-riffic plants in the garden, the cost of harvesting their flavor-packed flowers and leaves falls to almost zero. Yields increase over time.

teas for two or more

LOOK THROUGH THIS LIST of plants, all of which are easy to grow and use for making teas, and then picture any or all of them in your garden. If you're not acquainted with these gems, you might want to begin studying up on their charms (see descriptions starting on page 204).

- Bee balm
- Camellia
- Chamomile
- Chicory
- Cinquefoil
- Citrus
- Red clover
- Evening primrose
- Fireweed
- Goldenrod
- Liatris
- Mint
- Passionflower
- Rose
- Stinging nettle
- Wild geranium
- Yarrow

Why, there's something for everyone's yard on that list! Flowering plants that grow in damp soil and shade, marvelous blossoming vines, plants that do well in patio containers, wildflowers for thin soil, and wildflowers for full sun. Wildflowers can behave perfectly well in the garden if tended carefully and not allowed to, you know, go wild.

Despite their diversity in height, hue, and form, these plants have a strong presence — whether in fragrance, brilliant color, intriguing pattern, or other characteristic. Many of them spread easily and can function as spectacular groundcovers even in difficult conditions. Some are naturally heat-resistant and drought-resistant, and, filled with aromatic oils, naturally pest-free.

We urge you to see what grows best in your own garden and then learn to make teas from those plants, rather than setting your mind on some variety in particular that may be unrealistic at your location. That said, one of the attractive features of herbs and wildflowers like these in the garden, including roses, is their toughness and adaptability to darn near any climate in North America. Not all roses are fussy: Depending on the cultivar, roses can thrive along a foggy New England seashore, high in the Appalachian Mountains, or in the sunbaked Southwest.

Where garden teas are concerned, the ingredients hide in plain sight in the well-designed drinkable landscape, disguised by bright ornamental clothing. One of the benefits of grooming herbs and wildflowers in the garden is taking cuttings several times in a season, in many cases, or harvesting roots throughout the year.

The more often you remove spindly stems and deadhead these plants, the higher will be your productive yield.

And we can say without hesitation that adding any of our tea-like plants to your landscape will reward you with bursts of beauty and with increased pollination all around the garden, thanks to beneficial insects their blooms will attract.

There's a wide world of tea made from the leaves, flowers, or fruits of various garden plants. Indeed, writers have produced books galore on just those subjects. But it doesn't take a book to know that a warming or cooling cup of any kind of tea acts as a welcome treat most times of the day or night. Effects of teas vary according to the kind of plants you are sipping: some calm the nerves, some stimulate the body and mind, some fight colds and illness and infection, and some just taste and smell good. A tea made from herbs, rather than from the camellia plant famous as regular caffeinated tea, is called a *tisane* (pronounced "tih-ZAHN"). We're calling them all teas, for simplicity.

Over thousands of years people have poured water onto leaves and flowers and other plant parts to produce pleasant, even lifesaving, beverages. We can picture prehistoric people doing this just as well as we can visualize sophisticated Parisians or hip Californians doing the very same thing. The English have their cuppa and even call one of their daily meals "tea." Japanese connoisseurs perform an elegant and moving ceremony, called the Way of Tea, to prepare and drink this honored beverage. We would all do well to celebrate our enjoyment of tea with respect and affection.

Even the august *New York Times* has reported that on some Greek islands the residents live to great age with the help of this simple mixture for an end-of-the-day cocktail: a handful of fresh herbs in a cup of hot water, with a squeeze of lemon added. Ingredients for this tonic tea can include any of the local aromatic plants growing wild on the hillsides: dandelion, rosemary, marjoram, giant anise, or mint.

Enjoying a cup of tea can be a solitary pleasure or a shared experience, a way to reconnect with oneself or with friends. It's an escape from the pressure-laden business of the modern workday for a few moments, whether at home or in a high-rise office. Savor the experience.

FRUIT CUBES

When you make fruit juices, freeze a little extra in a couple of ice cube trays. Pack the cubes in freezer bags to store them. In addition to using flavored ice in cold drinks, you can melt one cube at a time to add to freshly brewed tea for natural sweetness and flavor.

making garden teas

HERB, WILDFLOWER, AND ROOT TEAS require proper harvesting time, proper preparation, and proper storage. Leaves and flowers alike are often used for so-called herbal teas, and in some cases roots are, too.

A rule of thumb is that dried plant materials are three to four times stronger than the same quantity of freshly picked components. You may experiment to find just the right quantities to use for a cup of tea or for a whole pot. One easy formula is to use a handful of fresh flowers or leaves (½ cup, or half as much, if dried) for a pot of tea; in cases when more or less is recommended, we note that.

In most cases, you simply pour boiling water over the plant parts and let them steep for 10 minutes or so. Strain through a fine mesh strainer into cups. That's how to make tea you want to sip right away.

The second method, called sunshine tea, produces a stronger tea that's good for iced tea or for sipping cold throughout the day. Simply stuff a quart canning jar with fresh herbs or use a handful of dried herbs (mixing varieties, if you like) and fill the jar with cold water. Cover and let stand several hours in the sun. Strain the tea into second jar. Either way, you can combine herbs, wildflowers, and roots to make especially healthful drinks, such as mint plus stinging nettle.

harvesting tips

In general, harvest herb and wildflower leaves just before the blooms emerge. After that, the leaves can become bitter or unappetizing. The leaves of mint varieties should be harvested in early spring, when they are sweet and tender. When using herb flowers for teas, harvest just as they are beginning to open and the flavor is most intense.

The time of day is important for harvesting: Ideally, pick early in the morning, after dew evaporates but before strong sunlight dilutes the aromatic oils for the day. If you are lucky, you may find perfect conditions after a nighttime rainfall that washes dust from the leaves. Washing herbs and wildflowers can leave them unnecessarily soggy and difficult to dry successfully. That's why dew or rain can provide just the right rinse for removing dust; you can simulate one with a gentle bath from a watering can.

Remove leaves or flowers that have damage from insects or disease, or that are broken. If you are using fresh plant material, go ahead and remove flowers or leaves from the stems and use immediately, but if you plan to dry leaves and flowers in order to keep them over the winter, leave them on the stems and dry them whole.

Wash roots carefully to remove dirt. They can be used fresh or be preserved by drying.

drying methods

Drying herbs is simple, but failure to remove enough moisture from plant parts can lead to mildew or mold, and then the herbs are useless. Once leaves and flowers have thoroughly dried, so that they crumble when rubbed between your fingers, they can be stored in airtight jars and kept in a cool, dark place for a year or two, depending on the herb, without any appreciable loss of flavor. Roots can be sliced or grated and then dried and kept the same way.

To air-dry herbs or wildflowers, tie bunches of the stems with a string or rubber band and hang them upside down in a clean attic or in a room with a fairly constant flow of warm, dry air. A variation is bag drying, which simply means inserting the tied bunches of herbs into paper bags before hanging them; small shopping bags or lunch bags work well. Cut a few holes in the bags to promote air circulation, and label the bags. The advantage of bag drying is that herbs stay dust free and don't get messy if they crumble. Make sure there is room for air circulation inside the bag — don't overfill them.

A variation is room drying, which is especially useful for drying flowers for tea. For this method, snip off the blooms and lay them in single layers on several cookie sheets or trays. Leave plenty of space around each bloom for good air circulation. Cover the cookie sheets with cheesecloth to keep dust and bugs off. Don't stack the cookie sheets. Drying time varies depending on the material; it could be one to two weeks, but in very dry conditions less than a week.

Mechanical dehydration uses electricity, and solar power uses the energy of the sun to remove moisture from the plants in a matter of hours rather than days or weeks. Follow manufacturers' guidelines for temperature and times for your electric dehydrator. Herbs generally dry at much lower temperatures than fruits and vegetables do, so don't mix batches; fruits and vegetables also slow down the process by giving up a lot of moisture inside the device.

storage

Once leaves, flowers, or roots are dry, pack them loosely into clean jars with lids, then label the jars and store them in a dark, cool cupboard. Crushing them will decrease the flavor intensity. Temperatures above 60°F can shorten the life of dried plants, so a pantry or other storage place away from the stove is best.

GREEN TEA, BLACK TEA

One attractive plant, *Camellia sinensis*, is the source of the delightful beverage we know as tea, enjoyed the world over for its pleasant flavor and stimulating effects, and for its healthful properties, which include, purportedly, the ability to prevent some cancers, fight heart disease and diabetes, and cleanse wounds and infection. Tea is a miracle plant, pure and simple.

But there are so many variations! White tea, green tea, oolong tea, black tea, even yellow tea. They all originate in the tender young leaves of the tea plant, varying significantly in color, taste, and texture depending on a host of factors. Our discussion here is merely an introduction to a complex subject — growing, harvesting, curing tea — and can't touch all angles. Whole lifetimes are devoted to tea knowledge, and we'd like at least to share some basic facts.

With a culture dating back thousands of years in the plant's native Asia, tea is remarkably easy to grow, harvest, and process in the temperate zones of North America. Thanks to the mail-order availability of young tea bushes, any gardener living where winter temperatures stay above zero can succeed with many types of tea in just a few years. For colder climates, we have experimented with Sochi Tea, a cultivar from the Black Sea coast of Russia, and find it needs no pampering at all to survive ice and high winds. The attractive evergreen shrub eventually grows to six or eight feet in height, with yellow-white blossoms opening in fall; *Camellia sinensis* favors acid soil with plenty of organic matter dug in, plus lots of sunshine and moisture.

Make Your Own Tea

To make tea from your own two- or three-year-old plants, do what professional growers do: snip off only the supple light-green leaves from the top few inches of each branch, usually twice yearly in the spring and early summer. Then see which variations of harvest season make sense for you.

The main steps in tea processing determine the color: from white, through a range of greens, to black, the final product depends on the degree of controlled oxidation and fermentation. White tea exhibits the least degree in this progression, black tea the greatest. Green tea is made without the fermentation step, but rather processed with wilting the leaves by steam.

STEP 1: HARVESTING. The flush of new vegetation all over the tea bushes signals the time to snip leaves.

STEP 2: WITHERING, OR EVAPORATION. Just as gardeners can dry herbs on trays, with plenty of air circulation around the leaves, they can begin the tea fermentation process by letting some of the moisture evaporate. At the same time, as leaf moisture decreases, oxidation begins to alter the flavor and texture from the fresh state.

STEP 3: BRUISING, OR LEAF MACERATION. Once about a quarter of the leaves' moisture has evaporated, it's time to roughly crush, fold, tear, or otherwise bruise the leaves to release more compounds into the flavor structure. This disruption can be done by hand or mechanically.

STEP 4: FERMENTATION, OR OXIDATION. Now comes a period of dry fermentation by low heat. Tea leaves develop their rich flavor in a complex interplay of variables: weather, degree of heat, agitation, enzyme action. The longer the fermentation, generally, the darker the finished tea.

STEP 5: KILL-GREEN, OR HEATING. The fermentation process is interrupted by applying higher heat. In olden times this step could even be done in a cooking pan or wok. Today, commercial tea processors use more complicated machinery to perform many steps.

STEP 6: ROLLING, OR DRYING. Rolling the tea leaves, still slightly damp, develops even more flavors, as compounds deep in the leaves continue to blend and develop with each other.

STEP 7: LOW BAKING. A final baking step, still at fairly low temperature, can finish the tea processing. Centuries ago tea was often formed into dense bricks for transport and sale.

OTHER STEPS. A specialty tea called yellow tea results from a step after kill-green, as the still-damp leaves are cooked in a closed vessel, or sweltered. As a final step, teas can be cured, smoked, or otherwise enhanced with added flavorings.

In all cases, failure to adequately dry, ferment, or heat the tea leaves can let rogue bacteria take hold and over-ferment them such that they are useless for consumption.

Preparing a pot of tea varies in different cultures. Just consider how differently the Japanese and English approach their tea, while Russians have still other tea-drinking habits. Learning the ways of tea makes an interesting study for a long, cold winter.

plants for making tea

HERE IS A SHORT LIST of herbs and wildflowers that are useful for teas and interesting in the garden, or easy to find along roadsides or creeks; never remove plant material from protected public wilderness areas without checking regulations or permit requirements, and respect private property.

Consult specialized herbal sources for more complete listings and for more detail about medicinal uses. **Warning:** Always consult your physician before taking any herbs as medication!

- **Bee balm** (*Monarda didyma*), also called monarda — a tall, moisture-loving mint relative. Process the leaves for Oswego tea (another nickname for the plant), or use the brilliant red flowers to make a delicate ruby red tea. Harvest the leaves and the regal, crimson crown-like blossoms in summer. The taste is minty-citrus, and may remind tea drinkers of Earl Grey. Like any mint, the tea can ease digestive issues.

- **Chamomile, German** (*Matricaria recutita*) — a lovely field plant which produces fragrant little daisy-like flowers that are good for aiding digestion and sleep. Planted from seed as an annual, this chamomile grows as a low mat of delicate greenery on moist, well-drained soil; be sure to sow seed almost on top of the soil, as it needs light to germinate. Dry the blossoms and use as tea, several teaspoons steeped in a cup of hot water. There are other chamomiles, including the perennial Roman chamomile (*Chamaemelum nobile*), which looks similar and is used the same way. Avoid using chamomile if you take blood thinners.

- **Chicory** (*Cichorium intybus*) — a wildflower with pale blue blossoms. Blooms can be used for tea; the dried root is ground and used as a coffee additive or substitute. Harvest the flowers in springtime, the useful roots in fall before all above ground growth disappears in winter. Medicinally, chicory leaves are considered good for liver health and digestion.

- **Cinquefoil** (*Potentilla recta*), also called five-leaf grass — a fuzzy, low-growing wildflower with medicinal qualities. June is a good time to pick, while growth is robust. The flavor is mild. The tannin-rich roots can be used as an astringent to stop bleeding. Roots and leaves, steeped, can be used to treat toothache and fever, and a tea of the high calcium leaves is purported to stop diarrhea.

- **Citrus** (*Citrus* species) — Dwarf varieties of oranges, lemons, and all sorts of other evergreen fruiting trees can bring year-round satisfaction, in the kitchen and in a landscape or patio setting. Fruits often ripen in winter.

204

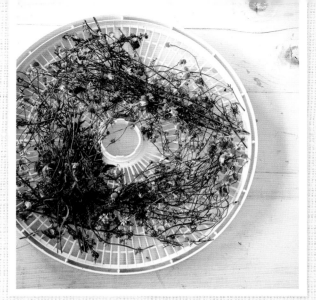

The flowers are creamy white and fragrant, and the slow-developing fruits produce both flavorful outer peels and vitamin C rich juice. Grow your own for pure chemical-free enjoyment.

- **Clover, red** (*Trifolium incarnatum*) — a bright groundcover. The red blossoms and bright green leaves are steeped for tea. This prolific plant seems to bloom constantly in hot weather and the flowers can be harvested anytime during the summer season. Excellent to dehydrate, clover has a fresh, delicate flavor like grass and is considered good for heart health.

- **Evening primrose** (*Oenothera speciosa*) — a valuable medicinal wildflower. The flowers really do bloom in the evening, generally in late spring and early summer, so harvest around that same time, before leaves get tough. A bit of honey can add interest, or mix evening primrose with more flavorful herbs or with fruit juice. Steep the leaves for 5 minutes in boiling-hot water and use to relieve stomach ache or cramps.

- **Fireweed** (*Epilobium angustifolium*) — a colorful wildflower that colonizes burned-over ground. Use the leaves for tea. Harvest the younger leaves in summertime for a pleasant, mild drink. Blooming in pale spires, fireweed is considered helpful in treating lung and breathing difficulties.

- **Goldenrod** (*Solidago sempervirens*) — a striking wildflower with many cultivated varieties. Make a tea from the leaves, flowers, or both together. The marvelous golden spikes bloom in the fall. Harvest then for use. Excellent in flavor, goldenrod tea was called Liberty Tea during American Revolutionary times and reportedly was exported to China. Considered a "heal-all," goldenrod tea has been used to settle colic and as a poultice for cuts and bruises.

- **Liatris** (*Liatris aspera*), also called shooting star — a handsome wildflower with spikes of lavender, white, or red flowers. The plant blooms in late summer in spectacular fashion. Tea is made from the corms (the rounded underground stem bases), and then used for colic, and the whole plant steeped as a tea to soothe overall body aches.

- **Mint** (*Mentha* species) — a prolific herb that comes in many flavors. Famous for "running" along the ground, mint can indeed become a pest if not managed in a walled area or in a buried pot. In the garden, mint favors damp and shady ground. Harvest before the blooms peak in midsummer in order to get the strongest flavor and aroma for drying. Mint is good for combining with less flavorful herbs. A tea of mint leaves calms the stomach and aids sleep.

- **Passionflower** (*Passiflora incarnata*) — a climbing vine with beautiful flowers. Harvest in mid to late summer. The flavor is mild and pleasant, much like the flower's fragrance. Use the leaves sparingly for tea, which is considered mildly sedative; try only a teaspoon or less of the dried leaves.

- **Rose** (*Rosa* species) — both petals and hips, the pink-orange autumn-ripening fruits, contribute to the drinkable landscape. The beauty is undeniable, the pollinating effect stupendous, and the nutritional value, of the hips at least, is nearly unsurpassed in nature. Dry the constituent parts for long-term use; the strong tart flavor of the hips needs to be tamed with honey and some hot water.

- **Stinging nettle** (*Urtica dioica*) — a moisture-loving springtime wildflower rich in vitamins and minerals. Used widely as a tonic, the plant should be harvested in early spring and summer before the flowers bloom, being careful to avoid the stinging hairs. They can leave welts for a few minutes, but country folks treasure this plant for its bright flavor and high nutritional value.

- **Tea** (*Camellia sinensis*) — This is, simply, tea, the beverage we know and love as a steamy cold-weather companion and hot-weather ice-cold friend. Yes, tea can grow in many parts of North America. The complete life cycle — cultivation, harvesting, curing — is complicated, but it can be a fine hobby for gourmet gardeners.

- **Wild geranium** (*Geranium maculatum*) — a low-growing wildflower with pale purple flowers. A spring-blooming plant, wild geranium likes woodland conditions: moist and rich forest soil and dappled shade. Harvest in spring and early summer. Use the powdered dry root for tea, which is used to treat diarrhea and various other conditions. The rhizomes — root tissues — are high in tannins and act as an astringent to stop bleeding and ease sore feet.

- **Yarrow** (*Achillea millefolium*) — a wildflower considered a heal-all since ancient times. Steep the leaves to make tea. After the flowers open in summer, harvesting commences. The medicinal tea is somewhat bitter, so mix with a sweet herb or fruit juice. The disinfectant qualities are matched by its cold-busting properties.

garden teas

In addition to the herbal teas described in the previous pages, you can make lovely teas from citrus peel and rose hips. And then there's kombucha, healthful fermented tea that is quite easy to make once you get the hang of it.

CITRUS PEEL TEA, TWO METHODS
(page 208). Use the delicately flavored peels, either fresh or dried, of your amazingly tender and sweet homegrown citrus.

ROSE HIP TEA
(page 210). Nature's health drink, high in vitamin C, makes good use of your lovely fruiting rose bushes, especially the *Rugosa* roses.

KOMBUCHA
(page 212). A fermented but nonalcoholic beverage, kombucha has a faintly vinegar tang on the tongue and is easy to individualize with the addition of fruit juices or herbs.

citrus peel tea

method one: fresh peel

1 quart (4–6 servings)

PREP TIME: 20 minutes

INGREDIENTS

- 1 **quart filtered water**
- 1 **fresh organic lemon or other sweet citrus fruit of similar size**
- 1 **teaspoon sugar**

1. Bring the water to a boil. As it heats, gently rinse the fruit to remove dust.

2. Use a sharp knife or peeling tool to remove the colored outer layer of the peel, being careful not to include any of the white pith underneath it. Juice the fruit and reserve 1 tablespoon; use the rest in another recipe.

3. Put the peel and sugar in a teapot or 1 quart canning jar. Fill with the hot water, and add 1 tablespoon of citrus juice. Let steep 10 minutes and serve hot, or chill and use as a cold drink.

4. For a single cup of citrus peel tea, use 1 cup of boiling water, ¼ of the peel, ¼ teaspoon of sugar, and just a squeeze of juice.

ONCE YOU GROW CITRUS TREES (often dwarf varieties, since many folks live in cities or in cold climates), you'll find there are numerous ways to use not only the delicate juice but also the peel that protects a tangy treasure.

One method is to use fresh citrus peel, cutting it carefully away from the bitter pith just under the colorful outer layer. Another method is to dry sections of citrus peel in an electric dehydrator or a solar-powered dryer and keep the peel in jars to use throughout the winter. Either way, feel free to mix citrus peel with regular tea leaves or with the leaves or flowers of other drinkable plants. Keep in mind that dried citrus peel is about twice as strong as fresh, and use accordingly.

Inhale deeply and enjoy the subtle mix of flavors and aromas (of course these are health drinks). Use organic homegrown oranges, lemons, sweet limes, blood oranges, and other sweet citrus fruits; grapefruit can work, but often is not as tasty.

method two:
dried peel

1. To dry citrus peels in a dehydrator, use relatively thick-skinned citrus fruits, especially sweet types; those with thick rinds will dehydrate better. Homegrown citrus is the purest available, because you know exactly what has touched it, but store-bought organic fruit with no color added to the peels is all right.

2. Rinse the citrus gently to remove dust. Use a sharp knife or peeling tool to remove the colored outer layer of the peel, being careful not to include any of the white pith underneath it. The peel may be in long strips or shorter pieces.

3. Spread the peels on the trays of a dehydrator. Follow manufacturer's instructions for temperature and time to process, generally about 135°F for 1–2 hours, until they are dry enough to snap in two.

4. Store dried peels in clean airtight containers in a cool place.

5. To make tea, use several pieces of dried citrus peel per teacup or mug. Heat water to boiling, pour over peels in a teapot, canning jar, or mug. Let steep 10 minutes to release flavor. Add sweetener to taste and drink hot.

Cook's Tip

For a taste treat, add half a cinnamon stick per cup before steeping.

rose
hip tea

INGREDIENTS

Ripe rose hips, at least 1 cup

Filtered water

1. Rinse the rose hips, and remove stems and dried ends.

2. Place hips in a saucepan, and cover with filtered water. Bring to a boil, then simmer, covered, for 40 minutes, adding water every 10 minutes to keep the hips covered.

3. Pour hips and water through a strainer or sieve and reserve the liquid. Press the hips through the sieve and reheat the resulting paste with the reserved water. Discard skins, seeds, and pulp.

4. Simmer the paste and water for 10 minutes, stirring to dissolve the paste.

5. Remove from the heat and strain the liquid into jars through a double thickness of cheesecloth.

6. Refrigerate for up to one week, or freeze in small batches to prolong useful life.

A simple way to make mild rose hip tea is to put a small handful of clean ripe rose hips into a saucepan, cover with 1 cup of water, and boil for 5–10 minutes. Strain and add honey or sugar to taste.

THIS DECOCTION OF ROSE HIPS is used not as a sipping tea, necessarily, but as a way to boost vitamin C or ascorbic acid content of other foods. You could turn a large harvest of rose hips into a high-C liquid. Likewise, because rose hips contain so much more vitamin C by weight than oranges, this tea provides a good way to bump up vitamin C for people with colds or flu.

Harvest rose hips right around the first frost. Before that, the hips may be unripe and hard. Look for the brightest red or orange hips, and squeeze them to see if they are starting to soften. Then pick.

1 cup to 1 quart, depending on quantity of hips processed

PREP TIME: 2 hours

Cooks Tip

Use any of the syrups from chapter 6 to flavor a sipping tea made from ¼ cup rose hip tea and hot water.

making kombucha

WE OFFER THIS PROCESS because kombucha only costs pennies to make at home, whereas store-bought kombucha costs a small fortune. From a health standpoint, kombucha's unique blend of probiotics and antioxidants produces glucaronic acid, the same substance the human liver makes to detoxify the body. To use as a tonic, drink 2 fluid ounces a day.

Although it may look like a fad drink, kombucha's origins go back thousands of years. Although no one knows for certain where it originated — Japan, China, or somewhere else — most of the stories refer to the concept of "fungus tea" made from seaweed or mushrooms. The elixir of life, the ancient ones called it.

Kombucha relies on a symbiotic colony of bacteria and yeast (SCOBY), also called a "mother" for its prodigious and long-recognized powers. You can obtain a kombucha SCOBY by purchasing a "live" kombucha drink and growing your own mother from it, or by buying a mother online. If you can't obtain a mother from someone you know, it's best to buy a mother that comes in enough liquid to begin your own process. The dried ones must be rehydrated with vinegar or commercial kombucha, which can be tricky.

Every time you make a new batch of tea, the kombucha mother will make one or more "daughters," which become mothers that you can share with your friends. The initial cost runs from about $10 to $20.

step by step

The following recipe makes about 2 quarts of kombucha. The active prep time is only about 30 minutes, plus 1 to 2 weeks for fermentation. Here's everything you'll need:

- 2 quarts filtered water
- 1 cup sugar
- 8 black tea bags, standard size
- 1 SCOBY, plus 1 cup of SCOBY liquid (the liquid the SCOBY comes in or a cup of fermented tea)
- *Optional flavorings:* herbs, berries, fruit juice

Heads up: Kombucha doesn't taste like wine or tea. It has a sharp flavor that can be tempered with the addition of different herbs or berries. Avoid herbs with strongly flavored aromatic oils, such as peppermint, sage, rosemary, basil, or bee balm. Instead, rely on lovely herbs such as anise seed, dandelion, elderflower, fennel, hibiscus, nettle, or rose hips. You can also use berry leaves and fruit.

making kombucha

1. To start, you need a kombucha "mother," one cup of the kombucha mother's liquid, and a container of two quarts or larger. You also need eight black tea bags, a cup of sugar, and two quarts of filtered water. **NOTE:** Always use filtered water, as the chlorine in some tap water supplies may be enough to kill the SCOBY.

2. The first step is to make a strong tea. Dissolve the cup of sugar into two cups of filtered water that have been brought to a boil. Add the tea bags. Cover and steep for about 10 minutes. When steeping is done, squeeze the teabags and pour the hot liquid into a clean half-gallon crock, mason jar, or other container. Add enough room-temperature filtered water, up to two quarts, to cool the tea and fill the container, leaving enough room to add the cup of SCOBY liquid and the SCOBY. **NOTE:** If the tea is too diluted, there may not be enough sugar for the SCOBY to eat, and mold could form.

3. Cool to room temperature. Pour one cup of SCOBY liquid into the container.

4. Add the SCOBY to the container (see page 214 for instructions on how to divide the mother). It may float on the liquid or sink; either is fine. After a few days the SCOBY will grow to take the shape of the surface of the container. It should be shiny and pale, and there should be no visible signs of mold. If mold is present, throw the whole batch on the compost heap.

5. Cover the container with a piece of cheesecloth, sheets of paper towel, or a clean dishcloth, and secure the covering with a rubber band or piece of string. (The same goes if you're using a mason jar — the point is to allow oxygen in while keeping out dust, bacteria, and other unwelcome visitors.) Place the jar in a dark spot, or wrap it with a towel to shield the SCOBY from light.

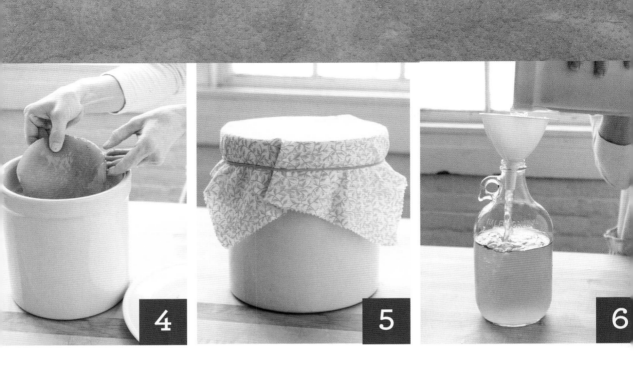

After about one week, start testing the liquid under the SCOBY with a spoon. The liquid will be slightly sweet, with a pleasant vinegar taste. Slowly, the sweetness will be replaced by the vinegar. If the liquid sits too long, the flavor becomes unpleasantly sharp. The idea is to stop the fermentation at the right point by bottling the liquid. Typical fermentation time is 7–14 days.

6. When the kombucha is ready to bottle, remove the SCOBY and transfer 1 cup of the liquid to a clean jar or bowl (this becomes the starter for the next batch). Strain the remaining liquid to remove any bits of the mother, as these can cause fermentation to restart. If desired, stir a ½ cup to 1 cup any fruit juice, or a handful of fresh or dried herbs into the remaining kombucha. This is the flavored liquid you will bottle.

Pour the kombucha into containers. You can use swing-top bottles for smaller servings or a half-gallon carboy (leaving some headspace) if you plan to drink it fairly quickly. Let the containers sit on the kitchen counter for three days or more. Check for the desired effervescence (bubbles and a slight popping when bottles are opened), then refrigerate. If you prefer less carbonation, refrigerate the containers immediately. You can also pour the kombucha into beer bottles and cap them, in which case, you must refrigerate them to reduce the risk of the bottles exploding.

Kombucha can be stored in the refrigerator one to two weeks, or longer. The longer it is stored, the more pronounced the vinegar taste may become. You can always add more fruit juice to counteract the vinegary flavor.

dividing the mother

1. Remove the SCOBY from your previous batch of kombucha and place it on a clean plate. You will see layers, like a stack of thin pancakes. With your fingers or using a spoon, fork, or other utensil, separate the layers for each new mother that you want to make. The SCOBY is firm and pleasant to touch, not slimy!

2. Pour 1 cup of kombucha with each new mother in a jar. Don't seal the jars; cover them with cloth so that oxygen can get in. These mothers, with their already fermented liquid, can be added to brewed tea to start new batches of kombucha.

Kombucha
mother
floating in tea

KOMBUCHA TROUBLESHOOTING

- Always use nonreactive pots and bowls when making the tea for kombucha.

- Don't skimp on the sugar, which is for the SCOBY to eat. If the SCOBY does not have enough to eat, mold will grow on the top, in which case the whole batch is ruined and must be discarded.

- Don't use flavored teas during the fermentation process. Some flavorings are not organic, and some are even antibiotic and antifungal, which could kill your SCOBY.

- Make sure your tea is lukewarm before adding the SCOBY. If the tea is too hot, the SCOBY will die.

- Be sure to cover the top with something breathable, like a double layer of cheese-cloth or paper towels.

- Don't start checking the tea until at least 1 week has gone by. Let the SCOBY do its thing before you disturb it.

glossary

AIRLOCK. A simple plastic device that fits onto a fermentation jug to prevent bacteria and wild yeast from entering the vessel and allows pent-up gas to escape.

ASCORBIC ACID. Synthetic vitamin C, used in canning to help preserve bright color and flavor.

CANNER. A large, lightweight cooking pot fitted with a lid and a low rack, used to immerse canning jars in boiling water for sterilizing contents and creating a vacuum seal.

CARBOY. A stout glass fermentation vessel with a wide body and a narrow neck.

CHEESECLOTH. Loosely woven, undyed fabric used for straining juice. Widely available in grocery stores and fabric stores; may substitute loose muslin fabric.

FERMENTATION. The chemical interaction of yeast and sugar in a liquid medium.

LUKEWARM. For winemaking purposes, temperature of liquids between 100°F and 105°F.

MASON JAR. The generic name for a tempered glass jar made for home canning, sold under various trade names.

MUST. The unfermented mixture of juice, yeast, and other ingredients that go into a carboy for fermentation.

PECTIN. The natural substance which helps solidify fruit juices, causing haziness in juices and wines; can be cleared with other natural ingredients, and often settles when juices are left overnight.

PITCH. To add activated yeast to a liquid to start fermentation.

PRIMARY FERMENTATION (see also Secondary fermentation). The active first stage of fermentation as yeast consumes all available oxygen in the must, followed by secondary fermentation as yeast converts sugars to alcohol.

RACK. To siphon off a fermenting wine or other beverage from the dregs, the decaying yeast and other fermentation byproducts, in order to clear it and help it continue fermenting in a clean container.

SECONDARY FERMENTATION. The quiet second stage of wine and mead fermentation, a period of weeks or months during which yeast converts sugars to alcohol and expels carbon dioxide gas in tiny bubbles.

STUCK FERMENTATION. Primary fermentation that suddenly stalls, requiring further action to keep the process moving.

YEAST. The micro-organism that consumes sugar in fruit juices and other sweetened liquids, turning the sugar to alcohol and releasing carbon dioxide gas.

YEAST NUTRIENTS. Natural compounds that help yeast start reproducing quickly to get fermentation under way, ideally grape skins left over from pressing, otherwise available from brewing supply stores.

metric conversion chart

Unless you have finely calibrated measuring equipment, conversions between U.S. and metric measurements will be somewhat inexact. It's important to convert the measurements for all of the ingredients in a recipe to maintain the same proportions as the original.

GENERAL FORMULAS	
Ounces to grams	multiply ounces by 28.35
Grams to ounces	multiply grams by 0.035
Pounds to grams	multiply pounds by 453.5
Pounds to kilograms	multiply pounds by 0.45
Cups to liters	multiply cups by 0.24
Fahrenheit to Celsius	subtract 32 from Fahrenheit temperature, multiply by 5, then divide by 9
Celsius to Fahrenheit	multiply Celsius temperature by 9, divide by 5, then add 32

APPROXIMATE EQUIVALENTS BY WEIGHT	
U.S.	Metric
$1/4$ ounce	7 grams
$1/2$ ounce	14 grams
1 ounce	28 grams
$1^1/4$ ounces	35 grams
$1^1/2$ ounces	40 grams
$2^1/2$ ounces	70 grams
4 ounces	112 grams
5 ounces	140 grams
8 ounces	228 grams
10 ounces	280 grams
15 ounces	425 grams
16 ounces (1 pound)	454 grams
0.035 ounces	1 gram
1.75 ounces	50 grams
3.5 ounces	100 grams
8.75 ounces	250 grams
1.1 pounds	500 grams
2.2 pounds	1 kilogram

APPROXIMATE EQUIVALENTS BY VOLUME	
U.S.	Metric
1 teaspoon	5 milliliters
1 tablespoon	15 milliliters
$1/4$ cup	60 milliliters
$1/2$ cup	120 milliliters
1 cup	230 milliliters
$1^1/4$ cups	300 milliliters
$1^1/2$ cups	360 milliliters
2 cups	460 milliliters
$2^1/2$ cups	600 milliliters
3 cups	700 milliliters
4 cups (1 quart)	0.95 liter
1.06 quarts	1 liter
4 quarts (1 gallon)	3.8 liters

resources

Here is information to help you quickly locate sources of expert advice about plants, equipment for producing homegrown beverages, canning and fermentation techniques, and bottling and storage supplies. This list is not exhaustive; it is simply impossible to list every available source. Instead, we are sharing the sources we use most often and trust, whether to answer a question about canning or to buy specialty items that might not be available locally right away.

canning, food processing information

National Center for Home Food Preservation
http://nchfp.uga.edu
Based at the University of Georgia, the NCHFP is as close to an official canning site as there is in the United States. The center compiles findings of the latest food science research and translates them into easy-to-understand form. This site can answer any technical question about canning, freezing, dehydrating, and other forms of food and beverage preservation.

plant information

Cooperative Extension System
National Institute of Food and Agriculture
www.csrees.usda.gov/Extension
The "Ag Extension," as it is fondly known, has offices in every state and can provide authoritative, localized growing information about any food or beverage crop. To find help close to home, click on the state map feature; in many cases there will be a county Ag Extension office near you. Local agents know about local sources of fruiting trees and shrubs and much more.

The Herb Society of America
www.herbsociety.org
Lots of useful information available online, even for nonmembers. The society sponsors a range of herb-related events and has a beginners' guide to growing herbs.

PLANTS Database
National Resources Conservation Service
www.plants.usda.gov
Here's another official source, with state-by-state information about all sorts of plants, including information on plant hardiness zones, endangered species, alternative crops, and invasive or noxious plants, as well as thousands of images for plant identification and other educational uses.

plant sources

We use and trust these plant sources. Of course, always start your search close to home and if you don't find locally grown plants, consider these reliable sources of stock:

David Austin Roses
www.davidaustinroses.com
Headquartered in the United Kingdom, but sells internationally. Comprehensive rose selections for landscaping, pollination, and hips.

Gurney's Seed and Nursery Company
Greendale, Indiana
812-260-2153
www.gurneys.com
A full range of fruiting trees and shrubs.

Heirloom Roses, Inc.

St. Paul, Oregon

800-820-0465

www.heirloomroses.com

Super-hardy rose varieties for a wide variety of landscape conditions.

One Green World

Portland, Oregon

877-353-4028

www.onegreenworld.com

Fruiting trees, shrubs, vines, citrus, and much more.

Raintree Nursery

Morton, Washington

800-391-8892

www.raintreenursery.com

Fruiting trees, berries, roses, tea bushes.

growing supplies, organic treatments

Here, too, the list is endless, so we include a few of the companies that offer useful equipment for planting, maintaining, and harvesting plants in the drinkable landscape:

CobraHead LLC

Cambridge, Wisconsin

866-962-6272

www.cobrahead.com

A small company that offers innovative weeding and garden tools.

Gardens Alive!

Lawrenceburg, Indiana

513-354-1482

www.gardensalive.com

Organic yard and lawn supplies and equipment.

canning, fermenting, dehydrating supplies

Fresh Preserving

Jarden Home Brands

Daleville, Indiana

800-240-3340

www.freshpreserving.com

A one-stop online shopping and recipe site for the Ball Company, which sells all sizes of mason jars as well as all other canning supplies and equipment. See the store locater for retail outlets nearby.

Kombucha America

Point Roberts, Washington

360-989-9464

www.kombuchaamerica.com

A comprehensive site for SCOBY (Symbiotic Culture of Bacteria and Yeast) culture and other supplies.

Lehman's

Kidron, Ohio

888-438-5346

www.lehmans.com

Another massive retailer, Lehman's carries some of the large or bulky items used in beverage making: crocks, presses, implements, harvest tools, and more.

Nesco/American Harvest

Two Rivers, Wisconsin

800-288-4545

www.nesco.com

For electric dehydrators and expansion parts.

index

other storey titles you will enjoy

Backyard Foraging
by Ellen Zachos
Photographic profiles and harvesting information — including advice on safety and sustainability — for 65 surprising edible plants.
240 pages. Paper. ISBN 978-1-61212-009-6.

Brewing Made Easy, 2nd edition
by Joe Fisher and Dennis Fisher
A foolproof
great beer
instructio
104 page

Home
Infuse
by An
Over 130
combinat
big-name
272 page

Homemade Soda
by Andrew Schloss
Recipes for a spectacular variety of fizzy juices, sparkling waters, root beers, colas, and other carbonated concoctions.
336 pages. Paper. ISBN 978-1-60342-796-8.

Put 'em Up!
by Sherri Brooks Vinton
A comprehensive guide to creative preserving: bright flavors, flexible batch sizes, modern methods.
304 pages. Paper. ISBN 978-1-60342-546-9.

it
s Vinton
how to put 'em up,
eserve fruit, as well
30 cooking recipes
78-1-61212-024-9.

DISCARD

e
0.